The Language of Light

Golden Keys to Ascension

To Jackie

Korani

With all the love in the world

Korani x

Published in the United Kingdom by Korani Light Publications

Printed in the United Kingdom by Baskerville Press

Korani Light Publications
www.korani.net

Content copyright © Korani 2009

Photographs copyright © Fritz Curzon, 2009, www.fcurzon.force9.co.uk

A CIP record of this book is available from the British Library.

First printed 2009

ISBN 978-0-9564934-0-6

Contents

Introduction

This book carries an energetic signature, a blueprint, a Divinely-offered template, designed to remind you of the language that your soul already knows. The words it contains are keys to guide you in unlocking the indelible codes written eons ago by your soul. The words are carriers for the Language of Light and I invite you to open to the unique transmission of energy carried upon them and to allow it to speak directly to the very core of your being.

This book is not a 'how to' or a set of answers or an instruction manual for the Ascension process, though it offers tools, techniques and exercises which you may choose to connect with. More, it is a journey of discovery woven from golden strands that you are invited to explore in order to find your own answers as you travel the Ascension pathway. What you are offered is a set of Golden Keys with which to unlock your own inner gateways. May they assist you in discovering the gold that awaits you there.

My truth, offered in these pages, is that we are all aspects of the Divine, in and of ourselves inherently, innately and perfectly part of the oneness. All that you find here flows from this, but I invite you to discover that which rings true for you and to leave that which does not.

If you let it, this book will change you as you read it. It will impact you on a personal, physiological, emotional, energetic and spiritual level. Enjoy the interaction it invites. Welcome the shifts as they take place; they are a signal to you from your own Divine light. May this book be a means for you to discover the perfection of this journey in all its myriad forms and seeming complexities. May you ride the Ascension waves with joy and discover the simplicity that comes when we remember the language of our soul, the Language of Light.

This book is a core component of the *Golden Keys to Ascension* programme that Melissie Jolly and I have developed together. It is also part of an Ascension Pack that includes golden Colour Mirrors oils which complement and enhance what is set out within its pages. It can be read alone but will be enormously graced by the use of the oils so that to read it without having them will be to miss an extraordinary opportunity. I wish you joy, whichever road you travel.

Details of the Ascension Pack and the *Golden Keys to Ascension* programme are available at www.korani.net and www.colourmirrors.com.

You may also like to join our online community: www.goldenkeys.ning.com.

Beginnings

Did you dare to consider that you are the creator of all around you, that you are literally following a thread, a trail that you have left for you to find?
~ Louise Langley

It is still early morning but the heat haze rising from the ground indicates something of the day ahead. Half a day and half a world away it is snowing and my body is slightly shocked at being dropped into a dusty, heat-soaked village at the foot of gentle mountains, the sky wall-to-wall azure. As I make my way to the southern-most tip of Africa my bones and molecules, on ice from a long English winter, begin to thaw.

Arriving in Stanford, home of Colour Mirrors founder and creator, Melissie Jolly, I am struck by Melissie's house, with its air of a small pale lilac angel perched at the top of the village. I feel its energy gently buzzing, humming, as though it could and indeed probably will at any time raise itself off the ground and take flight.

Walking into its cool interior I am met with a wash of golden light. Arrayed before me are swathes of golden oils bottled and ready for….well, what they are ready for I will find out. I have walked into liquid silk. My pores and cells open to receive the rush of gold. I have never before met anything quite like this.

I am here to spend a week with Melissie, my visit planned several months before, though neither of us then had any idea of the true reason or purpose of it. In inimitable universal timing, just days before I arrive, Melissie receives a message. Her guidance comes through loud and clear: there are to be seven new Colour Mirrors bottles; Gaia bottles, bottles to connect us with the Earth. But these will not be copper like the existing Gaia bottles in the range; these are to be golden, a Divine and inspirational gift to guide us into the new golden era on the new golden earth. I can hardly believe my luck. I will be there for the birthing of what we have already realised will be a new, dazzling power pack: seven delicious dual-coloured bottles, each with a pale gold fraction, which together form an Ascension set.

Melissie and I very quickly come to understand that these new golden bottles are something quite other than anything we have yet come across. For several days we cannot take our eyes off them. We sit in the shade of the terrace gazing at their sun-soaked beauty, feeling, exploring and discovering them, quite unable to tear ourselves away. We are steeped, infused, immersed in their energies. They seep into our consciousness and into our cells. Together we discover pattern and order within the

7

gold and that there is a journey which they will take us on, a guided and inspired journey into our own Divine essence.

Melissie calls these Golden Gaia oils the crown of Colour Mirrors. We know that they are keys, keys to a whole new way of being, of living, of experiencing. We know that they are gateways to the infinite possibilities of who we already are. These golden globes of Divine light offer us keys to Ascension. They take us through the portals of our beingness, on a journey that is at once a progression to ever-higher levels of consciousness and a return to the still-point of our essence where there is no need of a destination. We have been given seven Golden Keys to Ascension.

The Golden Keys present us with gateways and we know that we can choose to go through them, or not. We also know that we will come to know ourselves as we explore. And as we follow the path that unravels before us it is not an end-result we have in our hearts, it is the sheer joy of the journey.

Colour Mirrors

The story of Colour Mirrors, or Colourworks as it was known for the first seven years of its life, has already been told by Philippa Merivale in her wonderful book *Colour Works*. It is not the place of this book to tell the story again but rather to add another chapter. Like everything to do with the Colour Mirrors system, this book has become part of an organic process which evolved apparently spontaneously, unplanned and unbidden, yet somehow called forth, as always, by the system itself and the Divine Source that overlights it.

What is Colour Mirrors?

Colour Mirrors is guidance, inspiration, support and information. It connects us deeply, fully and swiftly with our inner selves. As the name suggests, it mirrors to us exactly what we hold inside; what we fear, what we love, what we hide from and where we shine; who, in fact, we are.

It is a system of colour and energy to raise our vibration, accelerate our growth, unlock our potential and recognise our magnificence. Taking us deep inside our own light and potential, Colour Mirrors is exactly that – a glorious mirror. It shows us, gently but honestly, where we have been holding ourselves back and then lights the way for us to take our next steps. It also shows us the truth of our innate beauty and light and asks us to see ourselves as we really are, reflected to us by the Divine. Each of the many glorious coloured oils and essences that make up the Colour Mirrors system has its own inspired message. Together they enable us to open to a higher truth. They are gentle guides to the en-lightenment of our lives.

Colour Mirrors facilitates a reconnection of spirit with body so that we may truly act as channels for Divine love and authentic light, right here on the planet. With their direct effect on our energy bodies these oils and essences support us in making changes; they may even be a key to wholesale transformation. Immersing ourselves in their coloured magic we find the messages of the oils go deep. The encoded language they carry within them speaks directly to our cells, to our very DNA. One of their great gifts to us is their ability to bypass the conscious mind. We might think we want to change, grow, heal, let go but the mind has many tricks and tools with which to prevent us from doing so. When we massage the oils into our skin or better yet soak in a colour-filled bath, the potent messages of the colours seep through to our bodies and our cells. They ignite a process of cellular level clearance and transmutation of those issues we have been consciously or unconsciously blocking or resisting.

Each bottle has its own meaning, its own note or vibration. As we contemplate the exquisite colours, we will find some we will reach for, drawn as though by a magnet. Some we will love and want to devour, others will call us though we may not know why. Our choice of colours gives insightful information to guide, inspire and empower. The palette of colours we choose reveals issues, patterns of behaviour, potential, areas for development, past life patterning, hidden aspects of our psyche and, perhaps most potent of all, the truth of the light we carry within us.

The Language of Colour

Colour speaks to us – the whole of us – in ways we cannot always consciously understand. Colour relates to the deepest, most hidden part of our psyche and draws forth what is there into the light, so that we may see it, understand it and if appropriate, let it go. It also draws out and reveals to us our deepest gifts, our greatest talents and our richest qualities.

Colour provides context and shows us where our contrasts are. Colour touches in exactly and immediately to our stuff, our issues, our agendas. There can be no pulling away, no hiding, no resistance in the face of these potent coloured packages. They mirror to us, utterly, who we are, what makes us up, our contradictions, our inconsistencies. We can turn away, refuse to see what is there, but once seen the mirror image remains, draws us back until we choose the path of least resistance and face what we have seen. In that process we enable and enhance our own healing, growth and transformation.

The language of colour is the language of light, for without light, colour does not exist. Colour reflects back to us what we already know and who we already are. Connecting with colour enables us to understand and to remember. It guides us in the letting go of the veils, masks and covers we have placed over the truth of our Divine nature and recovers us, restores us to that truth.

Colour Brings our Divinity into Form

The fundamental questions we might ask ourselves cannot be answered by another, though that is often what we seek. Perhaps all of life is a question, our purpose here to explore, excavate, uncover, discover, recover the truths of our soul. The answers we find, the words we use to formulate them, are an expression of our beingness, drawn out through the soul into the conscious realm, yet they remain only symbols of the essence behind them. They remain an interpretation, not the essence itself. Only in the living can we find the answers. Only in the being.

When we come into contact with colour we translate beingness into form. Our choice of colours draws forth that which is within us already, perhaps unexpressed. Colour births into a form we can hold, see, touch, smell, recognise. Colour enriches our thoughts, our feelings, our perceptions until they come alive with the vibrancy and the potency of light. Here, we say. This is me. Here are my shadows, some of which have been hidden, even from myself. Here are my joys. Here is my vulnerability. Here is my strength, my courage, my response to life. When we forgo the mental processes of thought and word and release ourselves into the soul's energies we drop the pretences, the guards and the stories. We formulate truth through the simplicity of our soul's response.

The soul recognises at the deepest level in an instant what it takes the mind minutes, hours, days, eons to grasp. Colour reveals it to us. Something happens when we sit with colour – with Colour Mirrors. Words are used, we question, we explore, we discover; and yet all of that is just surface semantics. What really happens is that we change. Our cells reach out to the silent messages in the colour bottles and pick up corresponding frequencies. They make subtle - and sometimes not so subtle - adjustments, aligning themselves with the deeper truth of our being. What was impossible begins to become possible. What was heavy, blocked, clogged starts to dissolve and dissemble into liquid light. The event or situation that seemed so intransigent loosens its hold on us. The dis-ease we thought we needed disappears. The blocks and struggles we used to identify ourselves with fall away. Suddenly, we get it. It may just be a glimpse, a fraction of a second, a flash. But we see it and nothing can remain the same. We can't un-see it. And what we see, written indelibly, unceasingly and eternally is our brilliance, our magnificence, our utterly transcended selves. In the reflection of the light from the colour mirror we know ourselves to be Divine.

Colours Combine

Energy immediately shifts in our bodies as we sit with Colour Mirrors oils. Our bodies recognise the information held within them. Our minds may have little idea of what is going on but our bodies already know. They feel, sense and understand the rays of energy pouring from these bottles of radiant light. Faced with the sparkling array of dual-coloured oils, we are granted access to a whole palette of information.

Individual colours on their own offer insight, understanding and information. Colours in combination reveal even deeper information about our patterning, our psyche, our thought patterns and what we hold to be true. Colour combinations offer us options and choices. We can go this way or that. We can choose to embrace what is revealed and to move forward or we can refuse to see what is hidden there. We may at times find our courage challenged. Yet as we sit awhile longer we let these messengers steep their Divine wisdom beneath our skin and let them heal the fissures within our being.

Colour Mirrors reveals information about our essence, our being, our spiritual longings and our soul's quest. The interplay of colours within each individual bottle and the set as a whole reveals a great deal more than single colours alone. Together, in concert, they present us with a pathway and offer us a journey. All we have to do is be open to beginning this journey of discovery. The combination of gold and certain other colours in the colour spectrum offers us a solid and very real background against which to paint our lives. The seven Golden Gaia oils provide a colour-coded set of Keys that will set us on that path. These are physical, tangible manifestations of Divine light that we can see, smell, hold in our hands, rub into our skin and literally bathe in. They act as a bridge between the world of energy - intangible, indescribable, perhaps elusive – and the world of material form. Bringing them together we begin to realise they are simply aspects of the same thing. Spirit. Body. Energy. Matter. All of it the same. All of it Divine.

Hearing the Truth

We are encouraging you to step out the door and embrace the countless realities that are only a frequency or vibration away. Allow yourself to imagine travelling to the stars. Allow yourself to see energy in its different forms without an overlay of your beliefs. Allow yourself to imagine how music might look or how music might smell rather than just how it sounds. Allow yourself to stretch into a space in which you question your beliefs and how you perceive your life.

~ Peggy Black

Melissie makes all of the colour bottles in the Colour Mirrors set. Her South African home is an alchemist's labyrinth filled with bottles and phials of dyes, stock essences, purified water, essential oils. As she makes each batch of coloured oils she 'hears' when they are exactly right. Their note sounds within her and she knows just when to add more of a particular shade or scent. The bottles have always spoken to her in this way. They also speak to those who use them and work with them. Sound has always been inherent in these richly coloured gems. Each has a voice, a note, a harmonic tone and our bodies hear them and reverberate with them as much as see them.

The seven golden Ascension oils act like tuning forks. They guide us with their resonance, encouraging, opening and coaxing us into alignment with what we know to be true. They take us deep into universal silence, a silence that rings with sound and light, connecting us with the interlinking lines of light that encircle the galaxy, weaving us into the web of life.

Colour Harmony

The coloured notes of the golden oils come together to create a harmony, an accord of light, a symphony of joyous sound. Each on its own is a potent tool, a reminder, a wake-up messenger. Together, they are a melody of unity, of oneness, bringing us into wholeness. Through this book we will discover and explore each note, each sound, each colour combination, each Key. We will begin to listen to our own harmony, to open our ears to the sound of our truth, our light, our soul, and to experience the interweaving of our notes with the harmonics of the cosmos.

The seven Golden Keys of Ascension are a harmonic progression where each note sounds in perfect harmony, each has its place and all come together to create something beyond colour, beyond sound, beyond form, beyond the mind's understanding. Through the harmony of coloured notes we find unity, accord, delight. The parallel narrative strands of each note weave together to form a pattern that speaks to our very DNA, awakening dormant light codes and re-activating our cellular Divine memory.

As we ply our bodies with the coloured oils, as we soak in them in and let them soak into us, our bodies release that which no longer serves us, and take on the information, the light, the message and the grace of the Divine.

We are being prepared for Ascension.

Ascension

The Game

The process of rebirth and ascension can be viewed simply as the raising of the vibratory rate of the Earth and her children. It is embodied in the state of consciousness that knows the self as divine. In the course of this rebirth, you will experience your God Self, or Essence Self. In doing so, you will become fluent in a symbolic means of communication called the "living language of light". This vibrational language is the native tongue of your Essence Self. It is characterized by direct transmissions of light essence, vibration frequency exchanges, and light pulses that transform on a cellular level, assisting in the creation of your light body. It expresses through feelings such as ecstasy, transcendence, communion, and unconditional love, as well as through patterns, colors, tones, metaphors, and mudras.

~ Ariel Spilsbury and Michael Bryner

We know that in essence, in the core of our beings, we are Divine spiritual light. We have always been that and always will be. The trappings of a physical life have been part of our journey to self-realisation, a giant experiential game designed to enable us to dive deeper into the fundamental questions, "Who am I?" and "Why am I here?"

If we know ourselves to be Divine – perfect, whole and complete – what possible evolution is to be had? How can our souls grow and expand if we are already all that is? The answer lies in our ability to create. As Divine creators we have the capacity and the ability to form, shape and craft any sort of experience if it will serve us on our journey to know ourselves and the infinite Divine of which we are part. We seek to experience life, ourselves, the Divine in all its forms. We seek to know ourselves through being. As extensions of the Divine creative source, we thirst to know and to experience every aspect of our vastness. The experience of earthly human life, lived inside the limits of a physical, dense form of matter - a body - is one of the choicest gifts we could give ourselves. Already knowing what it is to be pure light, to exist only on the level of spirit, our quest becomes how to experience that pure light whilst embodied in physical form.

For the game to begin we must condense our light, descend into a deeper, heavier, denser vibratory form and incarnate into the physical realm. As we slip from our spiritual light-space into bones and molecules and muscle we deliberately draw a veil over our being, shutting ourselves off from the memory of the light-source we carry within. This experience is only valid if we don't consciously know who we truly are.

In form, without the consciousness of our divinity, we begin to create a new reality. Our creative powers are such that the 'reality' we create appears to us as not only very real, but as the only reality. Within that reality we create stories, dramas, experiences that allow us to explore life in all its infinite richness. We create horror stories and fairy tales and everything in between and we experience it all.

The Awakening

Our connection to Source, to the oneness of all life, is infinite and ever-present. It is and we are. As we incarnate into physical form and take on the density of third-dimensional reality that connection appears to weaken, to lessen, to become faint, less tangible, less real. Experience in a body teaches us that we are separate. Conditioning takes this belief and deposits it firmly into our cells.

The process of Ascension involves initially awakening to the broader truth of who we are, remembering that there is, in fact, a veil in place and that the 'truth' as we have experienced it in third-dimensional reality may not be the whole truth, may, indeed, not be truth at all. Something in our lives acts as a trigger, a key. It may come in the form of a wake-up call, a profoundly shocking experience, an accident or traumatic event. It may come as a gradual sense of dissatisfaction and disillusion with the 'real' world, a longing or yearning that goes deeper than mere wishing and that often grows stronger over time. However it happens, the moment we begin to remember, to know, we can't un-know. We can pretend to ourselves, for a time, but gradually the illusion falls away. We begin to 'wake up', to remember. Our connection re-ignites. We begin to re-engage with who we really are.

The call of the soul for the expansion and light of our higher awareness is the catalyst that guides us to free ourselves from the bonds of ego consciousness which would hold us in limitation, separation and pain. This newfound sense of remembrance can be both a gift and something of a challenge. At times we may wander, lost, in the bewildering new world we see before us. Things we thought we 'knew' no longer hold true for us. Foundations, concepts and beliefs upon which we have based our lives, begin to shake and tremble in the face of our new understandings. Our world, in short, may be turned on its head.

Karen Bishop, an excellent source of information on the Ascension process, lists numerous Ascension 'symptoms' on her website and in her series of Ascension-related books. Loss of identity, apathy, exhaustion, confusion, a sense of disconnection – these are just some of the possible experiences we may have as we travel this Ascension path. Yet, just as likely, we will begin to experience more joy, freedom, exhilaration, passion, expansion and a feeling of knowing deep within ourselves. Many of the 'symptoms' of Ascension come about because we are releasing and letting go of old, dense, limited vibrations, thoughts, beliefs and emotions and our bodies, minds and egos are having to cope with the shifting sands of our new reality. It may feel like a new way of being, but the truth is we were never disconnected in the first place, it only appeared that way. We play out the experience of separation only until we no longer need it. As we remember that we are the creators of this game we realise we have the power to change the rules, change the stories, change the outcomes. We begin to reclaim ourselves as conscious creators. We begin to know ourselves as Divine consciousness experiencing itself.

Ascension is the remembrance, the journey back to the light, the expansion into the wholeness we have always been. In past times, those who transcended lower vibrating energies and raised their own vibration to a level of pure Divine spirit could only do so by leaving their physical bodies behind. Ascended Masters are beings who have fulfilled their purpose and departed from the physical plane to reside once more as pure spirit. We, current masters in the making, are taking the game to a new level. We are doing it in our physical bodies; ascending, raising our vibration, taking on our full spiritual light – while still in physical form.

Essentially, Ascension is the raising of human consciousness. Ascension, in this lifetime, means becoming the vision we hold of our Highest Self, our fullest potential, living our truth and our light, here, on Earth. And as that vision continues to expand, so too will we. Ascension is a process, not a destination, not something to achieve. It is a remembering, a re-awakening, a re-alignment with our core, essential, eternal self, the self that remains unchanged and unchanging, no matter the stories and dramas we play out on the surface of our lives.

The game is coming to an end. Humanity is awakening to an ever-greater height of consciousness. We are beginning to live in and from our wholeness once more.

The Choice

Our soul opens the gateway. We choose what we will do, where we will go, how we will travel. Soul lights the way. We choose to follow it, or not. But Ascension is awareness, and from awareness we always know that we have choices. We are offered choices at every step on our path. Our entire journey here is one of free-will, of diverse options from which to select those which align with our truth. Ascension is a state of being where we are free to live on a moment by moment basis in a conscious awareness of our light, divinity and highest truth. This means we are also free to choose our beliefs, our actions, our words rather than acting out our unconscious patterns and conditioning. How we do so is a further matter of choice; there are many tools and techniques available to us and it is an individual choice as to which path we follow. The more clearly aligned we are with our higher, deeper, essential knowing, the more easily we will be guided to exactly that which will assist us.

Ascension is a process we are all part of. It is available to everyone. Indeed it is a choice at a soul level that every being is asked to make. Not everyone will choose to ascend. Some will make other choices which are perfect for their soul's evolution. But for many, whatever the challenges - and there will be challenges - the Ascension journey is so rich and rewarding that it becomes a delight and a joy and a journey not to be missed.

What is Ascension?

Ascension is entering the space of the heart and choosing to live our lives from its sacred expansive truth. Ascension is a state of unity consciousness where our awareness rests in the understanding of our commonality rather than our differences. Ascension is a place where our apparent flaws are recognised as an innate part of our ever-unfolding perfection. Ascension is the fine-tuning of our inner crystalline structures and the realignment of our energetic pathways. Ascension enables the forces of the magnetic world to re-align and cohere to a new pattern, a grid of consciousness, a network of light. Ascension is living in a state of such knowing that fear, doubt, worry or concern can have no hold. Though they may still arise, they simply pass by like transient travellers. They can gain no foothold for their illusory tales. Ascension is a return to the Divine template or blueprint of who we really are. Ascension is the light of our divinity unmasked and unleashed.

In its simplest terms, Ascension is spiritual evolution. We will never cease to grow, to explore, to expand and to evolve for this is the very nature of life itself. There is no 'there' to get to. Everything and all is already within us.

Ascension Living

So what does life look like as we rediscover ourselves? How does Ascension look, experienced from the inside? As we raise our vibratory rate, as the frequency of our being becomes ever lighter, more refined, more finely tuned, we begin to experience a greater sense of oneness and unity with all. We become aware of the profound interconnectedness of life and the web of light that engages everyone and everything. Our experiences begin to show us that nothing is random, nothing is separate; synchronicities abound. Our intuitive muscles strengthen and we start to simply 'know' what our steps are, where our path lies and what we would create with our new-born knowledge.

Life becomes simpler and we experience joy from the simple and the small, the here and the now, the ever-present moment that is. We cease to worry so much about what might come or to fret about what is past. As we live in the ever-unfolding Now moment, we are more present to life, we live it more fully, we honour it more generously. We open to appreciation and gratitude as keys to our life and begin to sense the profound cosmic pattern that underlies everything. Shame, blame and judgement feature less and less as we clear ourselves of past conditioning and free ourselves of the bonds of memory.

Joe Vitale, in his revolutionary book, "Zero Limits", speaks of Ho'oponopono, the ancient Hawaiian process which invites us to come back to 'zero' at every moment. Freeing ourselves from the limitations of what we have perceived as truth, based on the faulty ground of memory, allows us to be open and ready vessels for the inspiration that comes when we connect to the Divine Source and the Divine Self. As we travel the Ascension path, we begin to attain the 'zero' state more and more, continually coming back to the silence and stillness that is at our very core.

We begin to recognise our glorious true nature, our magnificence and our mastery. We honour ourselves and others. We shift our perspective and begin to experience life through our Divine Self rather than our ego self. We learn, explore, discover and find that the 'home' we have sought has resided within us all along.

As the veil thins, as we clear more and more of the fog that has surrounded us, we begin to see through new eyes; the eyes of love. Pure love. Love without condition, love without bounds. We begin to live from the heart, that engine-room, that power-house of unconditional love. From a place of unconditional love there can be no judgement, for judgement is simply an illusion that keeps us trapped in self-righteousness, hatred and intolerance. If all is Divine and we have simply come here to *experience,* what then is there to judge? What then is there to feel guilty for? If separation is an illusion, if we all are one, who indeed is there to blame? The releasing of judgement is one of the toughest challenges for a human mind and it is one of the most potent keys to the Ascension process. Stepping outside the mind and viewing from love's perspective may literally transform our lives.

This is a whole new game and we are learning its rules even as we create them. Opening to more of ourselves we find ancient, current and future wisdom merging within us. We think we have come full circle only to find that we are travelling a spiral and are reaching ever higher.

Certain light frequencies are available to us now that we could not previously access and they transmit themselves to us when the receptor sites in our energy fields are prepared and aligned to receive them. We embed them into our wiring and allow them to become fully connected so that we can utilise the information they contain. We match DNA code receptor site to transmitting frequency and all that we need to know, all the information, is downloaded, fully formed, straight into the heart. The heart is the decoder, receiving, translating, integrating, making sense of it all. The heart, in fact, just knows. This is why we are beginning to live from the heart. This is why it is becoming imperative for us to live from the heart.

We begin to find we can only do things that make us feel good, that resonate for us, that ring true. Anything else becomes intolerable or at best, pointless. We also find that as we follow our inner guidance from moment to moment, we stress and worry less, we no longer feel we 'should' or ought to be doing certain things. We glide on a stream of our own pure knowing that takes us exactly where we need to be at any given time and brings to us exactly that which we need, perfectly on time and in tune with our higher wisdom.

As we raise our vibration we begin to radiate more light. That light reaches out into the cosmos, lighting up the gridlines that encircle the planet, connecting each living element in the universe to one another. We literally contribute to the crystalline network of light by increasing the amount of light that we shine. Our thoughts and our consciousness offer up a higher vibratory tone so that the very galaxies begin to resonate with a higher frequency. Ascension is not just a personal process. We are very much in this together, we, the Earth, the beings of light on other planes who support, encourage and guide us and the creative Source and light of all that is.

We might think we exist only on this dimension but we are multidimensional beings experiencing life from a multitude of platforms. As we step along the Ascension pathway we begin to have multidimensional experiences, to see, hear and feel our other dimensional aspects. We begin to realise how limited our third-dimensional 'reality' has been as we expand into the knowledge of our limitless souls. Separation becomes unity. Division becomes oneness. Life becomes love. Earth becomes Heaven. A new era dawns.

Code-Breaking

Is life just a code to be cracked? And if so, who determines the code? What if we ourselves are the creator of the code, the code itself and the code-breaker? What if life's truth was genetically programmed into our DNA?

How exciting does the game become then, if we determine the code by the very essence of who we are, by our very existence?

What does it mean for us if we are both creation and creator, experience and experiencer, divinity and Divine, conscious being and consciousness itself?

Golden Keys to Ascension

No book, no oil, no tool or technique acts in isolation. We are the most important factor in our Ascension process. The journey is, as always, up to us. Yet the golden Colour Mirrors oils show us the possibility of a new way of being on Earth, offer us keys to a new reality. The Golden Gaia oils and the words and energy transmissions of this book together make up a set of Golden Ascension Keys that can quite literally – if we allow them - show us who we are. They are the inter-linking components of a much greater dynamic than our conscious minds at first might allow.

The soft silken oils, infused with light and colour, smooth the Ascension pathway and offer encoding at a cellular level. This book carries transmissions of sound and light, energetically reconnecting us with the blueprint of our innate Divinity. Together, book and oils, colour and sound, information and energy offer the possibility of reconstruction of our very make-up, a reconnection to our eternal selves, duality coming into oneness.

Seven Coloured Keys

I first saw these bottles on the internet and as I looked at them I felt a "pull" inside. I knew that it would be a privilege to work with them and that things would change for me, even before I knew anything about them. I love the pale gold colour that runs through them. To me, this colour has always carried an angelic vibration and when they arrived I could feel their energy in my room. The gold began to glow as time went on and I could see an auric glow around them. I was mesmerised.

~ Diane Buckley

In the seven Golden Gaia oils we meet a template of colour. Gold, of course, is the under - or in some cases over - lying theme. But added to the gold of our seven Golden Gaia Keys we also have an array of shades: Turquoise, Blue-Lilac, Coral, Gold, Pink, White and Magenta. Each is in a particular place on the journey, in a very particular order. We will discover the joys of this Divine colour order as we travel, but for now, here is a glimpse of what they have to offer.

The first Key steps us into brilliant, beautiful turquoise, the colour that is intimately connected with the concepts of faith and trust. The Ascension journey begins, quite simply, with this one vital key: Faith. Why? Because without it, there would be no journey. The belief is the thing that moves us onto the path in the first place.

In Melissie's words:

"Without faith, who would even wonder about the God sphere? You wouldn't even go there if you didn't have the faith in the first place. It's absolutely the thing that moves all of it in a spiritual direction. Without that all the rest of it doesn't exist. If I have no faith, no belief, that's the end of the sentence, the end of the story, there is nothing more you can say to that."

Armed with faith and *Faith*, we take heart and courage and set our feet upon the pathway and the Ascension journey begins.

The second Key, *Impeccability*, takes us into the cool realms of blue-lilac where we begin to recognise the power of our word and our responsibility as co-creators of our lives. The colour here is a translucent, shimmering blue-lilac haze that can be read as neither blue nor lilac. It is something altogether other, leading us to wonder what might be there to discover in its mysterious light. It leads us gently into stillness, into silence.

As we emerge from the immersion of the second Key into the warm coral tones of third, *Generosity*, we begin to accept ourselves, becoming generous with who we are and opening to the beneficent light of the universe. The possibilities of gloriousness begin to stir in our bodies and we open to the resonant notes of joy.

In the fourth Key we step straight into pure gold and claim "I AM". I am Divine, I am love, I am whole, I am that I am. We claim our Divine selves, remember our authenticity, re-engage with our light and begin to live as our divinity.

From the fifth Key, the soft pink of *Grace*, we travel lighter and higher, softer and gentler, opening our eyes, hearts and minds only to love.

The sixth Key lifts us into the white, clarifying, purifying *Ascension Light* so that we might know ourselves as this light and in the process, release what is heavy or dark within us.

Finally as we dive headlong into the seventh Key we discover magenta and all the possibilities of Divine love, Divine being, Divine living. This is the transformative, transmuting, awakening power of *Satori*.

What we get with these Golden Keys, these physical, tangible tools of alchemical light is the opportunity to live and embody the qualities they embrace. They cease to be just concepts in our minds and become instead a bodily reality. So how, then, do we use these delicious golden oils? We can sit with them, hold them, delight in their light, dive into their beauty, enjoy their subtle energies and if we want to fully, utterly experience all that they can offer we will let their messages flow deeply into our marrow. We will steep ourselves in the healing balm of water, we will bathe in these heavenly sensual oils. Water acts as an energy conductor, carrying their divine and potent messages to our cells, bypassing the contradictions of the mind and going straight to the ever-listening heart.

Each Key is a state of being, one we are asked to explore and discover and align with before we progress to the next. Each Key builds on the one before, setting down a strong broad base before moving ever-higher, ever-lighter, ever-onwards. We appear to be travelling 'somewhere', to be moving up from one Key to the next, ascending the heavenly staircase. Yet we are also simply re-discovering what we already know, what already lies within us, and are travelling nowhere other than into the core of our own Divine hearts.

The Golden Journey

If you expect it to be perfect, then it is, every time. ~ *Melissie Jolly*

On my first day in Stanford I pick up a pack of Mayan Oracle cards and the card I draw is called Language of Light. These words and their energy resound deeply within me and through the course of the week ahead their significance becomes clearer and more and more profound. I understand that this is to be the title of the book I will write (and yes, to my surprise, there will be a book, and I will write it!). The language of our core essence is the Language of Light. The language of the Golden Gaia oils is the Language of Light. The Golden Keys to Ascension are reconnecting us with our mother tongue.

Sitting under the African sun, as I gaze at the golden bottles I feel both the sun and the bottles as connectors, as infusers. Plugging back into the solar light, the cosmic light awakens the sleeping knowledge from within my cells. The sun radiates light and as we fill up with its penetrating solar light, we radiate too. As we infuse in the golden colour bottles, steep ourselves in the wisdom, information, light and knowledge, we re-awaken to our magic. It is partly why we connect with these bottles, bathe in them, at least once or twice, perhaps many times. Each time awakens a further, greater level of light within us. They take the message deeper and deeper into the very marrow of our bones. We begin to radiate with that solar, cosmic, universal light.

For eight days, Melissie and I dig deep, going in, down, mining the gold. Yet at all times it feels utterly light. From the beginning we decide that as I am with Melissie for a week I will bath in one of the new bottles every day, that I will take the journey laid out by these Golden Keys. We know that the set of seven bottles is to become part of a guided Ascension programme where we will explore one bottle, one Key per week. Seven bottles in seven weeks sounds do-able. Seven golden baths in seven days sounds faintly alarming, yet also appeals to the part of me that likes to go higher, further, faster! Being 'at source' as it were, with Melissie's guidance and support on hand - not to mention a handy supply of bottles - and being intimately involved in the evolution of this set as I seem to be, it somehow feels completely right.

I duly begin the process on my first night but instead of starting at the beginning with *Faith,* the first in this new set, I know that I must begin and end the week with *Satori,* the gold/magenta combination which entranced me from the moment I set eyes on it. Having flown from England, a journey of nearly 12 hours, this is the combination I need to help me land - in Africa and in my body. It is also to birth me into the process that lies ahead.

The moment the magenta and gold hits my pores I am transported to a magenta planet. Bright starbursts of magenta light surround me and I am taken to a library, stacked with books. Together they contain the information of all that was, is now and will ever be. They hold all the wisdom and knowledge of the universe. I am being shown the Akashic records. I begin to wonder: could it be that these bottles are Keys to the hall of records? Within each of us is all we could ever need to know. Will the seven Golden Keys offer us entrance to the gateways that are already within, waiting to be re-discovered?

Day by day I follow the steps laid out for me by the bottles, these seven Golden Keys to Ascension. Beginning with turquoise and gold *Faith,* I feel as though I am being washed clean, cleared of all that has gone before so that I can begin this new part of my journey, free from baggage.

The next day's gold and blue-lilac *Impeccability* pulls up old feelings and beliefs for me to look at. Where am I not being impeccable with myself? Where am I holding myself back in the belief that small is safe? Key themes this bottle will touch on, as we are to find out.

Day three's coral and gold *Generosity* is sheer delight. Sensual and warm, it bathes me in a golden glow all day and shifts my mental gears into joy.

As the day of the fourth Key dawns, I know that this golden *I AM* has already begun its work and I sense subtle re-wiring and reconfiguring of my light

26

body. I am reconnected to the cosmos, my light grid strengthened and re-structured. The words I receive are 'preparation for Ascension'.

The gold and pink *Grace* bottle is utterly welcoming. It's warm and pure love comes straight from the Divine Mother. I spend a day in love with the world.

By the sixth bottle, the gold and clear *Ascension Light,* I am powerfully challenged. Will I truly step into my light? Can I really do this? The moment I get into the sweet, softly perfumed bath, all that flows is relief. Ascension is just another step, I am told. You already know how to do this. It is simple. So simple. Just surrender and let go. And from here emerges the clarity that begins to form the book you now hold in your hands.

By the second time I bath in the shimmery gold and magenta of *Satori,* eight days after the first, something has fundamentally shifted within me. I seem to have gone 'up' an entire octave. I experience bliss, joy and waves of expansive light, a ringing delight and a profound sense of gratitude. I am excited beyond belief at the possibilities unleashed by these golden Ascension Keys.

As my eight-day golden journey comes to an end I become aware that these new bottles can truly assist us in transforming and transmuting anything. Struggles, challenges, difficulties can all be transformed in the golden fires of their light. We have awoken a potent force indeed from deep within the earth. In this week Melissie and I spend together we feel quite hypnotised by these new golden oils but perhaps the Golden Keys actually reverse the hypnosis. We've lived under the hypnosis that we are stupid or undeserving or damaged or not enough or unforgivable, for long enough. These golden Ascension bottles remove that spell and let us feel again the magnificence of our true radiance. They take us into our golden core and unlock the door to the truths waiting there to be re-discovered.

Golden Keys to Ascension

As we walk with the colours and energies of the seven Keys we are offered an exquisite interplay of movement and stillness. One moment we are called to action: guided, inspired and in tune with our Divine note. The next we are asked to wait, to pause, to sink into the silence and allow. What we discover with these golden Keys is a progression, a journey, a map to our higher consciousness. The themes they engage us with take us further into our beingness, deeper into our subconscious and higher towards our light.

27

We begin this journey with faith because we couldn't begin without it. As we travel into impeccability, faith underscores our path. Faith underpins everything that comes after it, is a foundation stone for all that is to come. Impeccability prepares us for generosity. When we are impeccable with ourselves, true to ourselves, we are preparing the foundations for self-generosity and self-acceptance. We are not afraid to offer ourselves to others. Through generosity we discover what it is to stand in the light of our true being and this paves the way for us to claim our I Amness. In I AM, we are so filled with the truth of our divinity that we cannot not step into grace. From the simplicity and softness of grace, our Ascension Light takes form. And from there, it is but a step to satori.

In the Golden Keys to Ascension programme we spend a week with each Key, letting their messages speak to us, allowing them to unlock what is already within us and finding that they take us through gateways and portals to previously unexplored dimensions. We find that gold is an enabler, an accelerant, an activator. We discover that gold itself is a key.

What is Gold?

Gold is sunshine, lustre, preciousness, value, worth, wealth and beauty. Gold is flaxen, bright, lustrous, dazzling, resplendent, glowing and sparkling. Gold is blissful, joyous, flourishing, halcyon, prosperous, thriving and blessed. Gold is radiance. Gold is brilliance. Gold is alchemy. Gold clears and strengthens our aura. It assists us in manifesting abundantly and elevates our sense of personal power. Gold, like the golden stone, citrine, cannot hold on to negative vibrations. It simply disperses and dissolves them.

Gold is an amplifier. It magnifies wherever we already are, so if we are proclaiming ourselves as victims, our victimhood will be amplified. If we are ready to engage with our power, it will assist us in doing so. Wherever we are at, it meets us and mirrors us and shows us very clearly to ourselves. It also offers us new pathways, should we desire to take them.

Gold offers us to ourselves in its mirror. It reflects to us the truth of our light and divinity and it also holds up for us the places where we feel the need to control. Connecting with gold we become aware of authenticity, truth and power; we notice how and where they manifest in our lives.

Mining for Gold

As the golden Ascension set takes form, Melissie and I begin to connect more and more deeply with the gold that is in and of the Earth. We realise that indeed we are mining the gold to discover its value and preciousness, as we each mine our own gold to discover the brilliance that lies within us.

Melissie writes: *Gold. God with an L for love in it. The colour that surrounds the solar plexus and the colour for halos. This is where we find our absolute true connection to the source. Interesting if we think about the abuses that have occurred on this planet for the actual possession of gold. And all that the physical substance of gold can give us is what we have created in a misinterpretation of the thing we were actually looking for, which was heaven on earth. All the time what we were looking for was not kept in the depths of the earth waiting to be mined, but in the depths of ourselves, waiting to be mined. And waiting, to be claimed as MINE. I am what I am is the only thing I really possess and when I have that totally integrated in my cells, that is all I ever will need, as then the gold inside will be perfectly mined.*

Gold is true authentic power, the power that claims our divinity, and once that is in place, nothing else is needed as we have claimed our connection with the Creator. And as we are that, we are therefore as creative as our source, and manifestation is so completely our only right and our biggest possibility. Creation never stops and once we are connected to that energy we are also asked not ever to stop. In truth we cannot stop, as that is the force that creates everything. If we look with great keenness of vision at our lives we see that we have created everything in it. We did that. All of it. Now in the gold we can do it consciously. It is our only job. In the gold we hold our authentic power. It is also the colour that reminds us of the abuse of power when it is not the real thing. Every bit of abuse happened because of the loss of connection with the gold.

Our connection to the Divine is as much what we must have as our connection to our mother was necessary pre-birth. It is only when this golden energy centre is balanced that our lives have any real value. The gold is very hard to mine and it then has to be melted and treated before its value really appears. So often, to access the gold within, we also have to go through huge painful processes, but always at the end of the process we can claim more of our true value and live our lives from a point of true power.

The complementary colour to the gold is indigo and it is interesting that the Egyptians used equal amounts of lapis lazuli and gold in their head-dresses. Maybe it was to remind them that to access the power in the gold in an authentic way, they had to connect with the darkness of the indigo in the third eye and go inside where the true gold was. It was a message not to abuse the golden power but to retain the inner truth and make the power authentic and connected to the Divine self, not the outer self. Gold has pink added to yellow to bring love into fear and confusion. Love creates the potential for a golden age. Ascension finally, which is just another way of saying Heaven on Earth.

Golden Eagle

As Melissie and I begin connecting with Golden Gaia, the energy of the Golden Eagle makes itself known to us. We keep finding its image and its message coming to us as the golden energies grace us with their light. The Golden Eagle has been honoured and revered as sacred in many religious and cultural traditions and is a symbol of clear vision and freedom. With her ability to soar higher and see further than almost any other living creature, she represents our capacity to go beyond limitation and to see from a higher perspective.

Golden Eagle wisdom tells us that she is a solar bird, connecting us with the qualities of sun and illumination, lighting a path for our journey from darkness into the light of our being. She is a messenger of the gods, an emissary from the spiritual realms, come to enlighten our journey with her far-seeing powers.

I feel her energy as immensely generous and selfless, utterly connected to spirit and to the pursuit of truth. She encourages us to reach further, soar higher and to pierce the illusory clouds with clarity of vision. She brings courage, strength and grace.

Meditation: Golden Eagle Flight

Close your eyes and breathe gently into your heart centre. Feel the stillness and silence deep within your heart space. See it as a warm, dark place of great peace, a void from which, at the appropriate moment, life will spring.

Begin to become aware of your golden eagle-self, waiting patiently there, deep inside your being, deep in the inner chamber of stillness.

Feel the silent potential of its power, waiting for the moment you are ready to claim it. Pause in that space and allow yourself to feel the power mounting.

See the golden light of your inner eagle-self beginning to glow. See how she illuminates the darkness.

Feel her feathers, her wings, preparing to stretch, preparing for flight. Feel how the power and energy grows and accumulates, until it comes to a point of perfect readiness. And at exactly that moment she lifts off, spreads her wings and expands out of your heart chamber. Watch as she takes flight. Feel the joy of weightlessness as she effortlessly rises toward the skies.

Follow her as she soars. Let her bear you up to new heights. See the world through her laser-sharp eyes. Open your mind, free your limits, take the higher view.

Spend as long as you wish in this elevated space. See what you see with eyes that are unclouded by judgement. Feel what you feel in the openness of spirit. Hear what you hear in the silence.

When your journey feels complete, allow the golden eagle to bring you gently back inside your heart chamber and feel the golden glow she emanates there. Bathe in this for a moment or two, before allowing your breath to bring you gently back to the surface of your consciousness. Open your eyes when you are ready.

Gold Ascension Angel

Once the set of Golden Ascension oils settles into place, Melissie and I see how neatly the existing Colour Mirrors Angel essences match the new Golden Gaia oils and realise they will form a wonderful complement to the Golden Keys. The pale Blue Angel sits perfectly alongside *Faith*. Lilac Angel complements *Impeccability*. Coral Angel is an obvious match for *Generosity*; Pink Angel likewise for *Grace*. *Ascension Light* is enhanced by the Clear Angel and the magenta Metatron essence matches *Satori* in every way. But one is missing. There is no Gold Angel. It has to be born.

From the first it delights us with its radiance, its lightness of touch and its exquisite glowing power. We come to see that the Gold Angel in a very real sense overlights this Ascension Set.

Here are the words received by Melissie for this Gold Ascension Angel:

This angel essence is expansive and powerful. It balances the solar plexus instantly. It expands and solidifies your energy field and brings it back to its natural state, taking out all interference. It instantly connects you to your I Amness. Feel your feet on the ground and your light expanding as you breathe in this essence. It connects you to the new golden earth and it connects you to your Divine self. Here all is one and you are an integral part of all of it. As you expand into that, all fear and

31

confusion leaves and you are clear and powerfully present with what is. When you are this Divine and you claim it, all smallness disappears and everything you see reflects your authentic powerful Divine self.

All the Colour Mirrors essences* – Angels, Elementals and Dragons – are powerful supports for us on the Ascension journey. They gift us with immediate access to a higher perspective, opening our energy fields as they expand our physical and non-physical senses. The Angel sprays put us in touch with a softer, higher vibration. The Elemental essences engage us with nature and the subtle forces of the Earth. The Dragons show us the higher dimensional aspects of who we really are and connect us with the true power we hold. They offer a welcome added dimension to our process.

* For further information on Colour Mirrors essences visit www.korani.net and www.colourmirrors.com

Meditation: Becoming Gold

Spray some Gold Angel essence in your hands and above your head and breathe in its golden warmth. Close your eyes and invite the presence of the Gold Ascension Angel. You may see, sense or feel the light and the brilliance of this Golden Angel around you. Let the angel approach you. Experience its light as a laser beam of radiance enfolding you. Feel yourself melting into gold. Feel as your sharp edges soften, your pointed aspects become round, the jagged pieces of your energy field dissolve into liquid golden light. Become fluid, formless. Become golden light.

After some time, begin to feel your formlessness take form, a sacred geometrical shape or pattern that is unique to you. Feel yourself becoming that shape as you take on the energy of gold - power, authenticity, light, wisdom, brilliance.

Connect once again with the Gold Ascension Angel and begin to see now who you really are, your light, your purpose, what you are here to do. Let yourself see the truth. Let yourself be shown your unique and individual pathway that lies ahead of you, the journey you would create for yourself, inscribed in gold.

When you feel complete, take some deep breaths and bring your consciousness back to your present surroundings.

Gaia Transforming

Copper Gaia

Written in light, many eons ago, was the message of Gaia, the Earth's living essence. In times far distant, it was foretold, the Earth would undergo a major transformation. She would shed her density and step into a lighter wave form of energy whereupon the golden age would dawn upon her surface.

That time is now. Gaia is on the move. She is swiftly leaving behind all that is heavy, all that is of low-vibrating density. Many of us, of course, are going with her. We too are sloughing off our third-dimensional hindrances and stepping into the magnificence of our light.

Since the inception of Colour Mirrors, or Colourworks as it was then called, in 2001, the presence of Gaia in the system has been a significant one. The bottles themselves are rounded and generous like the Earth Mother, and not one but seven copper Gaia bottles have graced us with their warm, resonant earth-light. Each of the seven has been a connecting thread, guiding us on the journey to remembrance of ourselves as spirits in physical form. When, in 2007, a further Gaia bottle announced itself, it took us into an altogether unexpected place.

Into the Darkness

Darkness is the soil that germinates the seeds. It's the softness of sleep and the inspiration of our dreams. It's plush and fertile, the stuff of everything we use to sculpt our reality – most of our creations come from that hidden, unconscious place.

~Philippa Merivale

The Ascension journey really begins in the darkness, the void, the space of no–thing from which all is created. The earth herself was birthed from the dark splendour of nothingness. We took form from deep within the still, silent waters of the void. To journey into our light, we will surely have experienced our darkness. We would never have sought the light if we had not encountered the dark. We have perhaps gone through a dark night of the soul. We have probably encountered our own darkness in unexpected ways. Yet darkness harbours the light as surely as day follows night. If we are ready now to embrace and accept the darkness within us as part of the Divine whole, we can finally begin to claim the totality of ourselves. We can finally begin to journey homeward.

Across the Bridge into the Light – Illumination (G8)

The last Colour Mirrors bottle to be created prior to the golden Ascension bottles is the deepest darkest magenta, so dark that it looks impenetrably black. It's name? *Illumination*. It's purpose? To provide a bridge from all that we perceive as our darkness, to the full light of our truth. One of the gifts of Colour Mirrors is that it shines a light on the shadow aspects of ourselves so that we can find them, feel them, explore and accept them, thus integrating them into our wholeness.

And where do we find gold? Deep within the earth, in the darkness. We have to be taken into the darkness of *Illumination* so that the golden light can be born. We travel deep into the darkness to find the gold and in doing so we discover that the darkness is magenta. And the key that magenta holds? It is the gateway to Divine Love. It is the knowing and the understanding at the deepest depths and the highest heights that you are Divine and divinely loved and cannot be anything other. The shadow is also the Light. All of it is Divine.

The first of the Golden Keys, *Faith* (G9) - is the new, the cleansing breath, the fresh start. But we must come to this process with awareness of what it is we are beginning. We cannot begin this process with just another story, another drama. The Golden Keys will take us beyond illusion. They will keep ringing the truth and they will keep us ringing our truth. This is the New. We are crossing the bridge into a new dawn. All that no longer fits with our vast and unquantifiable light must be left behind.

The Golden Age

Much has been spoken and written about the coming of a new era, heralded by the ending of the Mayan calendar on 21 December 2012 when the Earth completes a 26000 year cycle and the sun aligns with the centre of our galaxy, the Milky Way. The 'Shift of Ages' as some are calling it, offers us the opportunity to live our higher vibrating light here on the Earth.

Many spiritual paths point to a Golden Age, a Satya Yuga, an Age of Truth, indeed the coming of Heaven on Earth, a utopian era occurring when enough inhabitants of the planet raise their vibration high enough to sustain it. What this will mean is the subject of much contention, discussion and debate. The truth is, we do not know for certain. All we can know is what our hearts tell us, what our souls guide us toward and what speaks to us as truth. Our entire existence is in a continual state of creation and evolution, so to state categorically that this or that may occur is to deny our fundamental creative nature. We, together, the inhabitants of the planet, have the capacity to create whatever scenario we deeply desire, so the story remains, as ever, up to us.

Gaia, the Earth herself, is certainly in a state of heightened evolution. She is shifting her vibration at a powerful rate and has been for some time. The 'shift' has already begun. As we lift our vibration and raise our light, we come together in love, the pure note of the universe, and discover that a new planetary matrix is being built from the combined hearts of all. We are on the threshold of a new Golden Age.

Seven Golden Keys to Ascension: Our Journey

What follows are the seven Golden Keys, each one set out to guide and enhance your own Ascension journey. In the *Golden Keys to Ascension* programme we connect with one Key a week for seven consecutive weeks in the sequence given, a sequence we have been shown again and again is a divinely orchestrated one. Only you can know how they will best serve you and your journey, however, so I welcome you to explore and ·discover what feels right for you. The programme itself offers a deeper process with additional guidance, support and material but my wish is that you will find that just connecting consciously with each Key through this book and the Golden Gaia oils brings its own rewards.

A few introductory notes will help to explain what is set out in the following chapters.

Each bottle in the Colour Mirrors system has a written description as well as an energy signature. The descriptions of each of the Golden Gaia oils, as received by Melissie Jolly, are included in italics at the beginning of each Key.

Where the name of a Key, such as Faith, is written in italics, it refers to the Colour Mirrors bottle of that name. Where it is written as simply part of the text, it refers to the wider concept or quality of that Key, including the bottle.

Each Key comes with a 'Harmonic' or energy transmission which is designed to facilitate your journey through the seven Golden Keys. Read the transmissions as often as you wish as you work with each Key and allow their energy to transmit the Keys to you on an energetic level. Some find that reading them aloud enhances their power and indeed recorded versions of the Harmonics are available to those who participate in the *Golden Keys to Ascension* programme.

Each Key has a number of "Keynotes" or themes to which it relates. If you would like to experience the full depth of what the Keys have to offer, explore these themes as you read. Open to what they have to offer you, ponder their meanings and their significance for you. Let their notes sound within you as you explore each Key and your experience will be all the richer and more rewarding.

For each Key we have collected feedback and insights from participants on the *Golden Keys to Ascension* programme and others who have been connecting with the Golden Gaia bottles and experiencing their qualities.

Some of their responses are offered at the end of each chapter to bring the Keys to life through personal experience.

The Language of Light is a potent, rich, sumptuous and expansive language. It will engage with you as much as you let it. This language will uplift you, shift you, guide and empower you. It may also challenge you. Take your time. Savour each Key, let its messages seep into your bones and your being. The Keys that challenge you can be the greatest gifts if you allow them. Do not resist those places where you feel challenged but instead dive in, explore, allow. You may find you want or need to be with a particular Key for some time before moving on to the next. Allow yourself that time. You will know when you are ready to move on by the call bubbling irrepressibly up from within you. Heed the call and step into your adventure.

Most of all, enjoy.

Faith

The First Key: Faith

When you walk to the edge of all the light you have
and take that first step into the darkness of the unknown,
you must believe that one of two things will happen:

> *There will be something solid for you to stand upon,*
> *or, you will be taught how to fly.*

~ Patrick Overton

Choosing Faith

I know as I'm writing this book that I need to connect deeply with each of the seven Keys and let them show me what they will. In preparation for the first *Golden Keys to Ascension* courses I will be running, I immerse myself in the Keys, one a week for seven weeks. Left-brainedly setting a start date to fit in with my other commitments I am blindsided by a deep dip of my usually high levels of faith and am plunged into beginning the process a week earlier than planned. I am being shown, as if I hadn't already got the message, that all things come in Divine time, not my time. It is, as always, quite perfect. I begin. I dream of bottles. I feel their golden lusciousness around me all the time, their potent energies working subtly in my energy field.

The *Faith* bottle itself is a delight. I find it warm, engaging, enriching and enlightening. It is cleansing, clarifying, enlivening; it feels almost like a purification in the waters. It acts as a detoxifier, releasing stale beliefs, old thoughts, denser energies. Its ringing turquoise and gold tones are amplifying and expansive and it shimmers and reverberates with bright sparkling confidence and optimism.

I am drawn deeply into questioning what it is, this thing called faith. I am also shown quite clearly what it looks like to live with it and without it. As I spend a week in the company of gold and turquoise *Faith* I continually draw my focus back to trust, to faith and I feel it returning and strengthening as I do so. It is as though this temporary setback is a test of sorts, designed to bring me into a more conscious awareness of my relationship with faith.

I sit with: 'What is faith?' and I am shown that it is a choice. I am asked to remember to step outside illusion and to reach constantly for knowing and certainty. I must continually choose faith until it settles over me like a second skin and becomes so much a part of me that I no longer have to seek it or even think about it at all.

41

Faith allows me to look beyond what appears to be real or true; it takes me into a higher perspective, beyond the stories I have told myself or others. In faith I need no proof, validation or explanation. In faith I can be, quite simply, with what is. As I contemplate faith I am shown that it is a means to freedom from fear, from doubt, from worry. If I know and trust and allow that all is perfect and all is Divine, fear and anxiety dissolve; shadows release; joy beckons. The sun is always shining, even when I cannot see it.

Faith gently earths and anchors me. It leads me into my centre, into stillness, into acceptance. It takes me beyond limited, limiting beliefs. Faith is the voice of my inner being, calling me ever onwards, ever upwards, ever heaven-wards.

In faith, I might finally let go of control.

I open my heart to truth and find that faith and truth are inextricably linked. I ask my heart: What is truth? and hear it ring within me as a high, clear, crystalline note. Truth rings. Truth is clear. Truth feels right; in fact it feels beyond right – it just is. It is a knowing and a calling and it resonates deep within me. I am true to myself when my heart shows me and I see, when it speaks to me and I listen, when it guides and I follow. Truth, I discover, is the language of my heart. Truth is the language of love. When I am not in truth I am not in love and when I come from love, truth is inevitable.

Truth is the bell that calls me on to this journey. I would not even know to begin without its tone ringing deeply within me. Faith is the means through which I access my truth. If I had no faith I would not follow the call of my heart, indeed would miss the call altogether. When truth rings it is faith that connects me with my deepest inner knowing and enables me to answer. The sound that faith and truth together make is a ringing chorus of delight.

The Journey Begins

Faith is a bird that feels dawn breaking and sings while it is still dark.

~ Scandinavian Saying

Welcome. Your journey is about to begin. And where it begins is in the clarifying tones of turquoise, the colour of faith, trust and the 'high' or enlightened heart. Turquoise is the opener, a key slotted gently into your heart chamber. You would not be here now if you were not ready and your heart knows it.

Trust.

Soft turquoise and pale gold *Faith* opens the door to your process. It states: "You are ready and you are come and now is the moment!"

Faith is complete trust and confidence and unshakeable belief. It is the knowing of the heart where no proof exists or is needed. It transcends the left brain and the rational mind and the need to control. Faith takes us into a soul space, an expanded space and all things become possible.

Bottle G9: Faith (Turquoise/Pale Gold)

As we move from the darkness of G8 we suddenly get a new vision. At the end of the dark tunnel there is a light and this light is turquoise and gold and indicates our new state. We are now connected to our authentic golden Divine power through our turquoise faith. It is the faith that moved us through the dark tunnel back into the light. Without the faith we would not have survived the dark night of the soul – in fact we would not have needed to go into it. It was our faith that took us there, knowing that there was another level, closer to the Divine, closer to our Divine selves. The turquoise over gold reconnects us to the flow and the trust that everything is on track and part of the Divine plan. It takes us beyond trust, and into the truth that we are Divine and that every thing we have experienced was Divine and therefore perfect. This colour combination indicates the teacher of the ancient truths in a new way. We are connecting to the golden age and are able to access the information of the past in a new way. This is the beginning of the opening of the hall of records.

Harmonic One: Faith

Your process begins. Your slate is wiped clean. You are offered a fresh start, a new beginning, a transcendent space. Cool, watery turquoise awakens you to the clarity and light of a perfect new day. Soft, pale gold opens a gateway to your light, your truth, your power. Together, they offer you the courage to take this journey, to take the first step. And the first step on the Ascension journey is Faith.

Faith is the catalyst. Faith is the anchor. Faith is the Key. Without it, you would never have begun this journey in the first place. But you have. You've sought and searched and yearned for answers and you are here, now, on the journey. It is your faith and your soul that have guided you here, clearing your path in moments of doubt, raising you swiftly onwards, lifting you gently upwards.

The turquoise of heart-knowing and the gold of empowerment clear the last vestiges of your fear like the sun dissolving morning mist over the sea. Together they offer you an opening to a new space, to a place that exists even beyond your faith. They take you into an awareness of the divinity in all that exists and you come to know yourself as that and to experience it in every moment. You move into integrity, the purity of your faith amplified and extended until it becomes knowing.

You are in integrity when what you know and what you feel are completely clear, completely aligned with your inner and outer truth. When you align with your wisdom and your feelings, your mind and your heart, any actions that spring from your integrity are then perfectly aligned with your truth.

Truth is clean and clear and unfettered. Truth rings. Truth calls. Truth resonates. Your body responds to truth as if it were a note that reverberates and rings through your cells. Feel the clarifying note of truth. On each step of your journey, listen for the ring of truth and feel it in your body and you will remain perfectly in alignment, perfectly in integrity. In integrity, you are exactly in tune. You sound your note of truth and it rings perfectly. You align yourself with your truth and you become it.

The only thing that can take you out of integrity, out of truth, is when you allow your faith to be dislodged. As you step out of faith, you step out of integrity. When you do not trust God, Love, the Universe, you have no choice but to do it all yourself and then you lose the finer sense of connection that links you to integrity. When you step out of integrity you can no longer hear your truth.

Your memories take hold. Memories of powerful past events that have possessed your body and your mind. Memories of "not enough". Memories of "wrong". Memories of incompatibility. Those memories have frightened you and you have stood back from the flames. "No", you have said. "I cannot do this again. I cannot take this journey". You remember all those times you claimed your power, spoke your truth, and died for it. "I am afraid," you say. And you step out of faith.

The memory of "not enough" has held you more than any other. It is the one you have all shared. And why? Because deep down in your collective memory you have played the game of believing that God is not enough. You have looked at your memories and you have felt the pain in your bodies and you have said: "Look what happened when I put my faith in God! Look where that got me!" God was not enough. God got it wrong.

And so it was all up to you. If God could not be relied upon, you would have to stand alone and face your memories and that too was a fearsome place to be. The 'not enough' had done its work. You could either trust in a God who got things wrong, or you could go it alone and trust in a You who could also get things wrong. The 'not enough' slid insidiously inside your psyche whichever way you turned. You and God. Neither one of you enough. You did not understand that the label matters not, that it is all but one and the same. Until you could utterly claim your faith, God would never be enough and you would always believe that *you* were not enough.

Then, in one dazzling moment of truth, you are offered another view, a slice of light into the darkness of your body memories. In a heartbeat, you are free. The light of your faith is restored. The dawn of a new day comes and it is time to reveal the light inside you as the greater power. Faith washes the memories from your being. You release them in a gold and turquoise stream of cleansing light. You recognise yourself as the powerful being that you are, you know yourself as a creator. You begin to see that you are God. The "not enough" passes out of your cells.

You claim your turquoise faith and the empowerment of your golden light and you feel the joy of the new Golden Age. You have journeyed through the dark gate and have travelled on faith as it led you into the light. You have become a way-shower, a teacher of the information of this new time on our Golden Earth and you are ready now to share your wisdom and your light.

Aligning yourself with your truth, you remember the information, the journey, the passage of your Ascension.

The golden sun shines on the turquoise water of the New Earth. A new era begins.

Keynotes of Faith:

- Trust
- Flow
- Cleansing
- Truth
- Integrity
- Acceptance
- Allowing
- Clarity
- Dawn of the Golden Age

As you journey through Faith, experience these Keynotes playing in your conscious and unconscious mind. Feel these themes running through your days, echoing and reverberating around your being. Roll them around on your tongue, play with their many facets and explore their unique meaning for you. Perhaps you will discover what faith truly is, for you.

How would it be to spend a day, a week, a month, a lifetime in faith? How would it be to be in trust in every situation? How would it be to never doubt for a moment that all is perfect?

Truth Rings

When our note of truth sounds and we hear and respond to the inner call of its resonance, faith guides our footsteps. Each time we trust in the knowing that rings deep inside ourselves we are given ever more reasons to trust. Each time we trust in our core of inner divinity and follow its guiding light, we experience whatever comes as perfection, no matter how it appears. We hear the bell calling us to action and we respond. Following the faithful truth of our heart-call, our action leads to manifestation. In faith, every outcome is perfect. But what happens if our desired outcome does not manifest? Will we use this as a reason or excuse not to trust again? Will we cling to the old, to our memories, to victimhood? Will we hold to the concept that life is something that happens to us? Will we interpret the non-appearance of our desire as failure? Or might we choose instead to see the perfection in the situation, whatever its appearance? Our desire may not, after all, be the greatest outcome. The timing might not be in alignment with our highest knowing. Perhaps there is something even more magnificent awaiting us than we could have imagined. As we release ourselves from the need to control we relax into the flow of faith. As we choose faith, we release anxiety. As we step firmly into faith, we let go of fear. As we open to perfect trust, stress and worry loosen their hold. In faith we flow on the turquoise river of life in a golden boat of trust and the glorious knowing of our creative divinity awakens.

Exercise: The Sound of Truth

With this first Key you are called to explore truth. You are offered the experience of discovering your own note of truth and aligning yourself with it. Begin to be aware of the sound of your note, to recognise it in your body, to hear it as it resonates within you.

Call to mind something which is dissonant to you, a thought or a situation that is disharmonious. Notice where its sound strikes in your body. Hear the tone it makes and become aware of your body's response to it. Become aware of what it calls you to notice, to see. Is there a truth here deeply buried? Is your discomfort a guide to a deeper truth?

Break state by standing up or focusing on something unrelated for a moment or two. Clear your mind, take some deep breaths.

Bring to mind something you resonate with perfectly. A project, a concept, a philosophy, a relationship, a job; anything that feels utterly right and connected for you. Notice where you feel that rightness, that truth, in your body. Notice the sound it makes. Hear its note. Let yourself bathe in the sound and feel your cells opening to it.

Get to know these feelings. They are your guide to higher alignment. They are your guide to your truth. Trust in this. Have faith. All is Divine.

Trusting Faith

With the Key of Faith we unlock the first gateway and behold those places in our lives where faith is not. Issues of trust and confidence are drawn to the surface. Where do we feel we have to do it all ourselves? Where do we feel let down? Do we even *dare* to trust? And why indeed should we?

Perhaps we like to over-control and take responsibility in ways that are not required or useful. Perhaps we prefer to renege on responsibility entirely. Both of these are habitual responses that deny faith. *Faith* invites us to notice our patterns, to discover the well-worn tracks we have laid down for ourselves and offer them into the turquoise and gold ocean to be erased by the waves of faith. Faith shows us that though we may experience pain it is up to us whether or not we experience suffering.

Our past experiences, conditioning and memories may serve to tell us that trust is a fool's game. Our bodies may remember the information from memories stored within them and call out for release. Past or present lifetimes of horror, abuse, persecution have held our cells trapped in memory. If we choose now to turn away from the pain, the memory remains, goes deeper, gets stuck. If instead, we sit, persist, allow, explore, dive into the body's response, we allow the memory to come, call it forth. As we wrap it in our soul's love and deep acceptance, allowing that what happened was the soul experiencing itself in all its divinity, the body begins to understand what that experience was and to recognise it as perfect. The body begins to know it is safe, always and forever, that the soul's infinite love cannot change, cannot diminish. In the face of faith, fear dissolves into that infinity. Through the penetrating beam of unconditional faith we are set free to roam the universe in all its vastness as a being divinely loved and divinely loving.

Releasing Judgement

Questions of faith have always arisen in every culture, every religion, every facet of life on Earth. We have wondered and questioned and explored and been told many stories along the way. We may have come to believe that faith is just a prop, a salve, a relinquishing of our innate divinity and personal power to a being somehow 'out there'. But does our faith really rest in a deity whose role it is to choose, with seeming sleight of hand, our fate? Is faith a delusion for those who would prefer to side-step a life lived in self-responsibility?

Exactly who or what do we have faith in?

The faith of which we have often heard speak has been a faith based on judgement: God's judgement of us for our sins; God's judgement of others for theirs; our God-given right to judge another based on the superiority of our faith, and so on. It has also been a place-setter at the table of God's guilt and the belief that if it weren't for God's guilt in the first place, we might just be able to forgive ourselves.

What the Key of Faith and the *Faith* bottle teach us is that true faith is both based in and comes from a place of no judgement. What Faith shows us is that without a guilty God, we become free to mine the depths of our own unconditional nature. When we can relinquish God from guilt, we can also free ourselves.

By turning fear-based versions of faith on their head, we connect with the faith of spirit, the faith that arises from love. We begin to know what it is to connect with flow, with trust, with allowing. We begin to see that love and acceptance for ourselves only comes through the portal of absolute and unconditional faith in our divinity; faith and trust that whatever played out, whatever role we took, whatever we appear to have done, it was never 'wrong'. The only way we or another can be wrong is if we persist in misunderstanding the truth, seeing things only from a limited map of the world.

Could we release ourselves from that weighty burden in the gentle light of faith? For what if it is in ourselves that faith truly rests? Whether we call it God, the Universe, Love, the Source, our soul, our higher self, our heart, our truth; the name does not matter. Fundamentally they are all the same. What if faith in ourselves *is* faith in God/the Universe/Life? What if faith in life itself is the ultimate and greatest key to freedom and empowerment?

When we have faith in life we choose a greater perspective, we no longer shrink from what is but embrace it and drink from it and taste and experience it. When we have faith in life we open ourselves to it and the experience has the richness of golden nectar. And what, after all, did we come here to do, if not to experience all that life might offer us; all that we as creative sparks of the Divine source itself might choose to create, to experience? As we step into faith we give up our stories of victimhood. Nothing is wrong, nothing is done to us, nothing is outside of love, nothing is outside of life.

Could we then release another from the same burden? If all was indeed in perfect Divine order, could we set free all the guilty parties in our story's long and colourful history and turn them over to a new dawn of freedom?

The answers to these questions come when we set aside our memories. Let us take ourselves beyond the memories and see, this day, from a new perspective. With a clean slate, what could be possible? From a 'zero' state, could faith grow a sturdy new bud?

The turquoise and gold of *Faith* is an opener, revealing a much greater perspective, a higher truth. With it, we can consciously choose to release our old inherited patterns. Faith allows. It opens us to a heart-knowing that goes beyond the mind's limitations and rules. The heart knows only truth, only love, only divinity.

Faith is turquoise, the colour of feelings, the colour of a heart that remembers its true purpose. When we simply think faith it remains a concept, a head construct, an idea. When we feel faith, we can live it. This Key is an initiator. It unlocks the faith that already exists within us, no matter how hidden, tangled or buried, and brings it into the cool clear light of day. With Faith, this first foundation Key, we begin the unravelling journey back to knowledge, to satori, to awakening, to the heavenly heart of life itself.

Faith allows an opening to the hall of records that we hold within our cells. All the information of all that is resides there. For many eons we locked the door to this knowledge and denied ourselves access to much that was there. Now it is time to begin to re-discover and re-activate the coded Language of Light that our body knows and understands. Faith and *Faith* are the keys that will unlock the door.

Meditation: Stepping into Faith

As you close your eyes begin to become aware of an energy, a flow, a cool turquoise stream of light merging with your field. Take some time to feel it.

Allow yourself to merge with it. Let it wash away anything that has prevented you from being in trust, in faith, in truth. But more than this, let it bring to you the feeling, the knowing, the sensing - or even just the possibility - of what it is to live in a world where faith is the path you tread.

Let a door appear before you, or a gate, an opening, an entrance. In your hand is a golden key, the perfect key for this doorway. And at the perfect moment, in the perfect way, with an ease and a flow of movement, see or feel yourself opening the door with your key. On the other side of the door is life lived in complete faith and trust.

Step through, in your own perfect time. Step into faith. Live it. Be it. Know it. Explore it. Here is your life, in faith. What does it feel like? Who is there with you? How does it look? What do you experience?

Spend as long as you wish exploring your life in faith. Envelop yourself in it. Discover its many facets.

When you feel ready, return to your present surroundings, bringing with you your vision and sense of a faith-filled life.

Time for Faith

At the end of my first week of conscious connection with the Key of Faith, I make a conscious decision to hand back to the universe the concept of linear time. Often in my life I've been stressed by time: being on time, finding time, making time, meeting a deadline, fitting everything I want to do into a given time. What the Key of Faith shows me, each time I connect with it, is that I can *only* be at exactly the right place at exactly the right moment. It cannot be otherwise. I recognise that time and timing are always divinely orchestrated and that in truth, I need have no fear of them as I open to the greater perspective my heart would always show me.

How might our lives look and feel without the shadow of time lurking? If we are in faith we know everything that needs to happen will happen in the perfect timing and the perfect way and we don't need to control, manipulate, arrange, shift or 'make' anything happen. This Key asks us to constantly bring awareness to where we are controlling and where we are in faith. We might recognise this by how much stress we are feeling, for stress is ultimately a lack of faith. Stress says if we are not in control, who is? Faith says the plan is working, it is all in hand - whatever the appearance.

"Zero Limits", the ground-breaking book by Joe Vitale explores the idea that we are either living from memory or inspiration. If we apply this to faith, we can see that when we are living from a memory, conscious or otherwise, we feel the need to control. When we are coming from inspiration we do what it is we're inspired to do. It's not that we stop doing altogether, quite the opposite. It is our responsibility to take action in our lives, no one else's. But, as Melissie says: "If we 'be' the thing we're inspired to be, the doing happens naturally." It's about letting go of faith-less doing and stepping into guided and inspired doing. Turquoise is the colour of water, of the sea, of the flow of life. When we are in faith we can let go. There is nothing we need to hold onto. When we are in flow we receive the inspiration we need to take the next step and we let go and ride the waves that overlight our consciousness.

Can we take faith into the minutiae of life? Can we walk faith in every second of our lives? The faith journey is most assuredly a spiritual one but it is also the most practical element of living every day in the deepest, highest connection with what is. We just can't 'do' heaven on earth unless we actually do it – be it - here, in our everyday lives.

This is not blind faith. It is a choice. It is a conscious awareness. It is a congruent heart-guided realisation. We must choose faith again and again and again in our lives until it merges with the guiding light of our own divine nature and we know it as intrinsically as we know our name. We must choose faith until it resounds perfectly within us, ringing out our truth.

Faith is the thread we pull through this entire journey, literally underpinning it all. When we are in faith this journey of Ascension can be both the most serious spiritual quest and the lightest soul adventure.

Faith in Action: What Does Faith Look Like?

One of my richest experiences of faith came in 2004 when I decided to leave my 'day job' to set up a healing and empowerment practice. At the time, my husband was half-way through a three-year training programme to become a nurse and was receiving a very minimal income. It seemed, on the face of it, to be a crazy idea for me, the breadwinner in the household at that time, to be giving up my full-time job to follow my heart. Yet I never faltered. I trusted completely and implicitly that things would work out. And of course, they did. I didn't just jump the moment the idea came into my head – it was something that had been building for a while. I also did my homework and my research and was completely sure that I was ready to take the leap; yet it still took an act of absolute faith. It was because my heart was completely engaged with this process that my faith did not waver. It was truly the only course for me by this time and I knew, simply knew, that it was the path for me to follow.

One of my very dear friends shows me by example how faith looks, in action. She lives every day from a place of absolute trust. Each morning when she awakens she tunes into her higher guidance and opens to the possibilities of the day. She has a family and the usual daily commitments of a twenty-first century life, yet she rarely plans. She listens to her heart. She picks each day as if it were a new and fresh fruit, ripe to be plucked. She follows spontaneously what her heart guides her toward and even in periods when nothing seems to be 'happening', she trusts that all is unfolding perfectly.

We can tell when people are truly faith-filled. They are those who trust their hearts, follow their guidance and open to the glorious resonance of their higher minds. They shine with a particular resonance not unlike the *Faith* bottle itself. They are lit with a higher purpose, guided by a heart-strong flame, carried on a tide of love.

Faith is greatest courage aligned with truest soul connection. Faith is the recognition of the Divine in all creation. Faith, ultimately, is perfect and total surrender.

Experiences with Faith

For me, connecting with the *Faith* bottle brings a high sense of excitement, anticipation and joy. It is as if it lifts a heavy weight and brings me into the light of potentiality and possibility that exist on all planes. Each time I engage with it, this bottle and the energies of faith bring me a focused clarity and a lightness of being; I hear the note of resonance running through me and it is true and bright, crisp and cool.

On a one-day workshop to introduce the Golden Gaia bottles to existing Colour Mirrors practitioners and teachers, each participant was given a bottle of Faith to hold and connect with. Almost all in the group experienced the energy of this bottle in their heart and/or third eye chakra. Given its turquoise energy the resonance with the heart was expected. The third eye connection was perhaps less so. But what we began to see as we explored deeper was that *Faith* brought us collectively into "seeing" through the heart.

I feel that I have cleared and cleansed some deep rooted issues. I felt quite emotional as faith touched my heart and allowed me to let an important part of my life move on. I am feeling the golden key turning in my heart and the feeling is very beautiful.

Christine

This bottle had a huge effect in terms of me trusting and not being held back by fear. In the last six months I have had a situation in my life where I had decided the only option was not to see a certain person ever again, as I was sure this would lead to big trouble for me. I thought that this was an end to the saga and had put it out of my mind completely. Then halfway through using the Faith bottle I suddenly found myself making arrangements to go and see the person in question. I was completely astonished with myself. By the end of the week, I had taken myself there and of course everything was fine. This was the most enormous leap of faith and it just happened. I really never thought that I would be able to do this.

Anne

This bottle certainly has the potential for the recipient to access the Akashic records. What I truly believe is that I could not have accessed the level of a pattern I have been in and its pernicious hold (and me allowing it) had it not been for the Faith bottle. Sure, I would have got there eventually but something remarkable has been happening, which I attribute to the access of the Akashic records.

Amanda

I woke up having seen the turquoise/pale gold Faith bottle in a dream. As I lay thinking about it, it came to me, an inner knowing, that to go forward (to ascend) I must leave the bags behind. I saw in my mind a hot air balloon, pushing sandbags over the side so that it could rise into the blue sky. I saw events all through my childhood, teens and adulthood when I had wanted to do things that would have stretched and challenged me. If I had done them there would have been excitement and exhilaration so why had I held back? I re-ran the events again from when I was a small child and heard again conversations with my parents. I was always presented with lots of "good" reasons why something should not be done. It meant that life was very limiting. I grew up thinking that this was how things were, lots of good reasons not to go somewhere and not to do something different. Never any good reasons to do something beyond the norm. I know that my parents' lives were not happy and I lived in an environment of anger and fear. On a soul level, I thank them for letting me experience this. It was fear, lack of faith and trust which held them back. For part of my life, this was my image too. I lived a lot of my life fearing what would happen if what I did failed to work out instead of having the faith to trust it would. Furthermore, not everything is meant to be a roaring success. It still has its value, teaching and changing us. It is not to be feared.

Diane

I ran a bath, and set up some music. I decided I needed some serious deep music because I needed to set the tone for this serious journey I was embarking on. I climbed into the bath, poured in about a quarter of the Faith bottle and lay there listening to the music. I felt a little uneasy, but interested to see where it was going to take me. The music changed but kept the tone and in that moment I realised that what I was feeling was fear. The whole thing had been about fear, fear of the group that I was joining, fear of committing to a 49-day process, and based on all the stories of what other people had been going through when they had bathed in the bottle fear of what was going to happen too. In fact I was so afraid of what might happen I had actually put off using the bottle. But it didn't seem right, I knew that faith wasn't fear. Also I had never used bottles over time, I was always the one who poured a whole bottle into my bath and saw what happened. I had let the fear of it all get to me. So with that in the back of my mind I grabbed the bottle and poured it all into my bath, took a deep breath and slid down under the water. The words leap of faith came unerringly to mind.

As I lay there under the water I realised that faith wasn't fear, faith was the voice in the dark guiding you, faith was the ledge that you land on after jumping off the misty cliff. Faith is life without fear, it's the courage to do it anyway even if you're scared.

I raised my head out of the water and let out the air I was holding and smiled, because in using the Faith bottle I had taken the leap of faith and as promised by the bottle, landed safely on the other side, ready to continue my journey.

David

Impeccability

The Second Key: Impeccability

Impeccability of the word can lead you to personal freedom, to huge success and abundance; it can take away all fear and transform it into joy and love.

~ Don Miguel Ruiz

Impeccability: Into Innocence

To be impeccable is to be faultless, unerring, unimpeachable. To be impeccable is to be innocent, sinless, without flaw. To be impeccable is to be who we really are.

In his powerful best-seller "The Four Agreements", Don Miguel Ruiz describes impeccability as meaning "without sin", where sin is that which goes against ourselves. We have been told that to sin is to go against God, but in the all-encompassing light of the Divine we know that, in truth, we and God are one. If to sin is to go against God, then it is to go against ourselves. Being impeccable, being without sin, means we can be *for* ourselves instead.

If we are innocent, we are without sin. If we are perfect, there is nothing to forgive. If we are impeccable, we are in alignment with ourselves. We can no longer be against ourselves. We are for ourselves. We are for life. We are for love. We are for all.

That way lies freedom.

Impeccability Calling

My days with *Impeccability* are soft, still, gentle. I sit with questions: What is impeccability? What does it mean for me to be impeccable? I discover that it means, simply, to listen. Impeccability means that I listen to and align with my essential Divine self. *Impeccability* - the bottle and the choice - gives me simplicity. It is high and light, it is pure, free and unencumbered. The silence of these colours keeps drawing me in and reminding me how powerful it is to sit, to be; to be still. I may only manage it fleetingly at times but if I stop, even for a moment, a space opens up for new inspiration to flow in.

I feel myself coming back to stillness and silence even when much is going on around me. The ever-present silence lies beneath the activity, the doing, the thoughts and actions of a day. It holds out to me a light that I can choose to ignore but when I take my focus there, even for a second, it quietens me, eases my mind, stills me and holds me gently in the moment.

I notice where I am being impeccable with myself and where I am not. I become aware of words I use that are not in integrity, actions I take that do not align with my knowing of who I am, thoughts that threaten to take me off on useless side-roads. I also notice where I hold true to my essence, where I listen to the impeccable call of my inner being and where I allow myself the glory of following the trail my soul is laying out for me.

Bottle G10: *Impeccability (Pale Gold/Pale Blue-Lilac)*

In the journey towards Ascension, this is where we connect with our impeccability. The blue-lilac says we speak our spirit and if that is what we are doing we have to be ever vigilant with our words. They have to be impeccable – we cannot use our words as weapons or instruments of manipulation. We have to speak with incredible integrity as we now know without a shadow of a doubt that everything we say will be made manifest. This bottle reconnects us to what we believe about the masculine side of the Creator and therefore the masculine side of ourselves as the Creator. It will bring incredible peace and put one into the silence and the stillness where the voice of inspiration within can be accessed.

Harmonic Two: Impeccability

You are called back into the knowing of your innate innocence. The colours of *Impeccability* call you to the truth and you know it. You are Divine, whole and impeccable. You are innocent.

Sin is perhaps the greatest illusion. You are God. All is Love. Where is the sin? To sin, to make an error, you must exist outside of the Divine, and that is something you cannot do or be.

It is only your memories that cause you to believe in something so illusory. When memories run your life, past conditioning, habitual seeds sown deep into the furrows of your being, you can never see what is right in front of you. Memory willingly guides you and shows you the path. Yet it is memory that leads you down dark and tricky lanes into the falsehoods of your own imagining.

Your creator self has no place for memories. Your innocent self hears inspiration and acts upon it. Your essence self lives on, from, and for inspiration. Your illumined light-being self lives impeccably every moment, hearing your note and attuning with it. Will you return to the child-like wonder of your impeccable self and stand in awe of the life that envelops you?

As you recognise your impeccability and your innate divinely gifted innocence the memories that have deceived you are cleaned. Every memory of error, sin and fault. Every memory of betrayal, deception and will for power. Your memories are no longer true and can no longer hold you or restrain you. You are free to step into the silence and hear the truth of your note without fear of the past. You catch the illusions of guilt and sin in your hand like butterflies and offer them up to the wind.

You are impeccable. Step into the silence and the stillness. This is the lull, the void, the space of allowing. Just pause and breathe…

In the silence and the stillness you hear the ringing note of inspiration from the Divine. Allow the harmonic of this note to sound into the silence and the stillness and settle into your being. This is the sacred space where you claim yourself, your tone, your note of truth.

In impeccability you are only being. Waiting, listening, still. Nothing arises until you are still. Coming to rest, you wait, knowing that the truth is already there. You pause as you await its unfurling.

Listen.

Allow. Pause. Breathe.

Inspiration arrives. The note of inspiration sounds and filters through to the whole of your being.

Inspiration is in-spiritation, in-spiriting, breathing, breath of life, the in-breath. It is the clearing of the memories, washing you clean and opening the space to new breath, new life.

The moment for action arises. You take a step. You fall gently into stillness, into the Divine void of expectancy. Stillness and silence; inspiration and action; stillness and silence. An ever-evolving symphony. A spiralling cosmic dance.

In the silence you hear your note of truth and it calls you now to sound it out, to speak it out, impeccably. As you speak your spirit your voice rings with truth, with impeccability.

You are re-learning the Language of Light, rediscovering it, beginning to speak it; you are rediscovering your voice, rediscovering the Divine within.

As your note of truth rings within you, your words become your truth. In hearing your truth and speaking your truth you blend seamlessly with the integrity that is you. You hear truth. You speak truth. You are truth.

When you are impeccable with your word you speak the Language of Light and you manifest in harmony with your truth, in perfect integrity. With your truth in place, inspiration comes, and you know it instantly because it aligns you. Your note rings true. You become your very own note of truth. You ring with the innate knowledge of your own Divine perfection.

In the still inner space you connect with your own true voice. You allow the will of the Divine and your own personal will to align. You discover that they are the same thing.

This is the space where your smallness, your doubts, your fears are challenged, held up to the light and seen through. Here is where fears of engaging your true authentic self arise and are offered up to the transforming note of impeccability within you.

Step into a balance of spiritual peace and joyous wisdom. Claim the empowerment of your spirit. All is available to you. You are the light and the joy and you emanate this in your beingness.

In gold and blue-lilac *Impeccability*, golden Gaia sits atop blue-lilac peace. The golden earth emerges now, for its basis, its foundation, is peace. We begin to live together on the New Earth, impeccably, innocently, in peace.

Keynotes of Impeccability:

- Innocence
- Stillness
- Silence
- Inspiration
- Integrity
- Alignment
- Peace
- Communication
- The Masculine

The Impeccability Key

We know already that impeccability takes us into innocence. We know that it guides us into stillness and silence and allows us to access the ever-unfolding gifts of inspiration. We know that it calls us to be in integrity and alignment with ourselves. The colours of *Impeccability* also connect us with issues of communication and expression. The blue of the throat chakra combines with the lilac of the crown, our spiritual centre, and we begin to speak with the voice of our unique Divine essence.

The subtle blue-lilac in the bottom of this bottle is reminiscent of the Colour Mirrors 'Gateway' bottle (No. 36). When combined with its almost-complementary colour, pale gold, an opening appears, the gateway to the next level, a higher vibration. These colours together clear away the story, the drama, the false and leave just the essence, the light, the truth. We are ready for peace, ready for balance, ready for harmony. From within the ringing note of silence and stillness, they arise.

Impeccability puts us in touch with our masculine side. We find with this Key that we are engaging with our male energy and watching how stillness opens us to movement, receiving leads to action.

As we dance with Impeccability and as we travel through this Key we allow its notes to sound throughout our being. We become aware of our stillness and our silences. We notice our restlessness and our noise. We experiment. We play. We observe. Above all, we begin to take ourselves lightly, impeccably.

Impeccable Silence

Memory is thinking. Inspiration is allowing. ~ Joe Vitale

We have begun the journey, the key of our faith has unlocked the first gateway and now we begin to explore. As we clear and erase the memories which once held us captive, we create a space for inspiration to flow in. The second gateway beckons.

This Key leads us to a place of silence and stillness, the allowing of a space where our souls can really reach us. We re-create the state of perfection, of innocence, from which we came. In the silence and the stillness we re-discover the innate innocence of all life.

In the busyness of our minds and our lives, how often do we pause? The noise inside our heads often prevents us from knowing our truth and hearing its note, but when we sink into silence, dive into stillness, it is there. A sound. A note. A tone. Speaking to us, if we would hear it. It's a moment by moment choice. We're offered it at every turn. The silence is always there, even beneath the noise. If we breathe, consciously, we will find it. If we take the laser beam of our focus into the silence we will discover that it lies beneath all, inside all, around all.

What is it like there? Will we pause long enough to notice?

It is into this still, silent space that Divine inspiration falls. Inspiration is a clear channel to the light and sound of the Divine without ego or will, memory or story clouding the connection. It is our openness and readiness to see the Divine, behold the Divine, hear the Divine, BE the Divine. Life lived from inspiration is the passport to freedom. As inspiration rings the bell of action calls to us and we effortlessly take the step that is there before us. Our actions spring forth from the stillness in a natural birthing of Divine energy. Rivulets of light issue from our being. We know and we see. We understand and we trust.

Impeccability, in essence, is utter simplicity. We release the need for complexity and confusion as it draws us into the ease of integrity and alignment. We discover that impeccability is not something to be gained or sought after, but that it is ever-present and already within us. In impeccability we release the perceptions and the memories that have stopped us from recognising our innocence and turn instead to the fullness of our inner, given grace.

Impeccable Integrity

Impeccability asks questions of us, calls us to stand in integrity. Where are we impeccable with ourselves? With others? Where are we not? What is our truth?

Our voice is longing to be heard. Do we dare to sound our note?

Impeccability asks us to acknowledge and express the truth and the light of our Divine authentic power. We are asked not to hide, to stay silent, to keep ourselves small. Our fears of being seen may arise; fears of expressing our truth in a world that has not, in the past, looked upon our views as worthy, valid or even permissible. Old worn-out beliefs and behaviours about what might happen to us if we lift our head above the proverbial parapet come creeping up to visit one last time. Will we give them our power? Or will we see them for what they are: memories of the stories we once lived but which hold no place in our lives now?

Gifts of Impeccability

Impeccability clears away the dusty layers of self-doubt, allowing us to emerge with focus and clarity about what we're doing and who we are. We begin to communicate and express our talents, our qualities and our consummate, innate gifts. We speak coherently, we act coherently, we become coherent, with a deep sense of our unique and Divine alignment and integrity. Self-doubt crumbles and falls away. We feel what it is to be aligned and in integrity with our own highest truth. We feel it in our bodies, deep within our bones. We feel what it is to live truth. Our intellect and intuition begin working neatly together in a dynamic and integrated partnership

With this second Key our voice begins to resonate with a higher truth and we realise that our words are carriers of power. We come to see that our words are extensions of our energy and that we can direct them with the potency of our light. We come to understand that our words can be used as beacons and tools and signposts rather than weapons of attack or defence. Our words can be emissaries of love if we let them.

The gifts of impeccability include potential for accelerated evolution and the ability to reach deeper, higher, broader, further than before. We are offered a clearer perspective, a higher view, a different frequency, a more empowered tone. As we claim impeccability we become a way-shower for others, a shining beacon, a bridge. Impeccability offers us the ability to emanate our light and our joy to others, simply by our beingness.

In the cauldron of gold and blue-lilac we forge our gentle inner knowing and our empowered learned wisdom. We can literally have or do whatever our souls call to us. *Impeccability* is a launch pad. It takes us to the next rung on the ladder, the portal to the higher dimensions. We are on our way to becoming all that we always were.

Attuning to our Frequency

As children we know instinctively what pleases us, what brings us joy, what we wish to embrace and where we want to be. Our feelings are finely tuned to our impeccable, resonant truth. Over time we begin to distrust our singular voice in favour of received wisdom, another's truth. We lose sight of what rings true for us. We forget how to receive the ongoing stream of guidance that flows to us incessantly from the Divine light of our own being. Turmoil and chaos, depression and disconnection arrive and we wander in these darker corridors for a time, wondering where the light has gone.

Slowly, as we awaken once again to the greater purpose of our lives, we begin to notice fleeting but laser-sharp moments of clarity and connection. We begin to tune in once more to our very own broadcasting frequency. If we practice and are diligent we begin to find we can hear the signals more and more easily. The more we listen to them the more swiftly and clearly they arrive.

Being impeccable means we are *for* ourselves and we listen, openly, honestly and intently to our own Divine truth. We listen to the note we are sounding. Where will we expend our energy? Will we take action now or will we rest in stillness? And if we are called to action, what choices lie before us? Where is our focus, our energy leading us? What resonates for us in this and every moment?

When we are impeccable we cannot ignore the feelings, images and lights of higher wisdom that flash, subtly or brightly, into our consciousness. When we are impeccable we are plugged in to our source and all that then comes is inspiration, truth, knowing. That knowing hums and sings within us, ringing throughout our being. Inspiration when it comes may be a raging torrent or a whisper barely heard. It may come as a vast sweep of light to guide us to our next step or as a subtle inner signal to choose one course of action over another. When inspiration comes we have the choice to ignore, resist or pretend it never happened or we can open to it, allow it, accept it, knowing it to be our truth.

When we pause, listen and respond we return to child-like innocence, to impeccability. Unimpeded by memory, conditioning or drama, we can reclaim each moment as it unfolds, rejoicing in it for its own sake, needing nothing beyond it, recognising its impeccable perfection.

The Impeccable Masculine

From the stillness of impeccability the key note that issues forth is inspiration, calling us to action, to movement, to an engaged connection with life. Here we connect with the active, dynamic tone of our masculine selves. We have heard the voice of our essence. Now we have choices as to where we might allow it to lead us.

In the masculine we find our ability to assert and construct, to organise and arrange. When we act from a place of alert and open receptivity, our inspiration lights the way for our actions to flow with ease, grace and simplicity. We balance and empower our dynamic tendencies as we listen, receive and respond. We have no need for struggle, striving or pushing. We have no need to 'make' things happen.

The colour blue connects us with our beliefs about the masculine. With its blue-toned base, *Impeccability* offers us the opportunity of coming to peace with the masculine in all its many forms; the masculine aspects of ourselves and our heavenly and earthly fathers.

What would it mean to experience the masculine in its perfect Divine essence?

In the warmth of Divine Masculine love we are resourced, protected and provided for, we are comforted, sustained and uplifted, we are supported, honoured and cherished. We are encouraged to step off the edge when we are afraid and supported as we take flight. We are bathed in the Divine light of the sun and it is safe to relax, to rest, to be still, in the knowledge that all is taken care of. We can just be. We are held. We are free to explore and to experience without fear.

When we fully embody this Divine male energy within, we become father to ourselves. Faith and impeccability merge in perfect harmonious communion.

Our focus shifts from fundamental survival to empowered joyful living.

Exercise: Embracing the Male

As you connect with Impeccability you are offered an opportunity to dive deeply into the waters of the masculine and find what you hold there. What does it mean to embrace the masculine, the male energy of the universe and of yourself?

The tri-fold energies of your father, God and your inner male are just reflections of each other, mirrors to show you to yourself. What are your beliefs about God? Is he absent, angry, abusive; or forgiving, all-loving, wise? How does this reflect your own father? Yourself?

Take some time to explore the male energies in your life.

Let yourself discover your own inner male. Begin to feel or see his energy. How does he appear? What is his energy like? Is he standing in his light, his power, his strength?

Does he support you? Is he available for action when you receive the intuitive nudge to move forward? Or perhaps he is hiding? Angry? Wounded? Lost? Discover what he has to say to you. His words are a key. Will you hear him?

What does your inner male need? What would make him whole? Give him whatever it is he needs. Watch as he gains strength, courage, power, light, wholeness.

Take some time to become impeccable with your inner male, your earthly father, your heavenly father, the men in your life.

What would you need in order to make peace with them all?

Impeccability in Action:

What Does Impeccability Look Like?

Melissie tells of a conversation she had with her son, David, who took the very first *Golden Keys to Ascension* programme with her. As she journeyed through Impeccability in week two, she noticed her judgements and then began to judge herself for having judgements, you know that old merry-go-round. What David said to her was, "Mom, don't be stupid. If you are impeccable, you are already perfect. Your judgements are perfect. Who you are is perfect. There's nothing to change. And all you have to remember is that whoever you are judging is also perfect."

She got it then. Impeccability is not based on someone else's perceptions of 'perfection'. Being impeccable does not mean being a saint. Impeccability is not a tool to use to berate ourselves every time we judge, or mess up or say something in anger. On the contrary it is a gift to guide us even deeper into ourselves, to align us ever more perfectly with ourselves, our innate knowing and our truths. It is in embracing the totality of ourselves, complete with judgements, 'negative' emotions and all our oh-so-human flaws that we become truly impeccable.

As we align more and more fully with our Divine essence, our inner light, we find impeccability calling us to flow, to glide, to delight in the river of life. I began to notice several years ago that when I really tuned into myself and followed my energy my life unfolded in peaceful, blissful harmony. I'd just left my full-time job to develop my passion for healing and energy work. Having received a bonus before I left I gave myself the gift of one month's complete freedom from "work" to just be.

I followed my inner nudges every day. I became acutely attuned to my inner guidance and followed where it took me from moment to moment. When my energy was flowing to a certain activity I was right there in it, aligned and connected. When my energy for that activity ran out, I felt it in my body and in my heart. That was the moment to stop. In the next moment, I would ask myself what would make me smile, what would feel just right, here, now? Would I like to snooze in the sunshine? Take a walk? Make a connection with someone? Read a book? Begin a project? Create something? Would I like just to be still, delighting in the unfolding moment before me? Whatever called to me, I allowed my energy to connect into the next moment and I flowed with it until it, too, ran its course.

I've never forgotten that month-long experience and have allowed its teaching to filter through into my life ever since. As my practice took off and I got busier and my life became more and more full, I would sometimes forget, find the connection less clear, feel less satisfied, less in joy. When I took time to be impeccable with myself, to be still, to listen, the flow would always come back.

I choose now to live in this way more and more. I'm better able to notice when something jangles and to shift my course of action, take another path, let go of whatever isn't working. I still have to remind myself and I don't manage it all of the time but as often as I allow myself, this is the path I walk. The clearer I become the more I allow inspiration to flow. I receive the call and I heed it. Inspiration rushes through me like the wind and carries me on a wave of graceful knowing.

As we follow our Ascension journey this call to live an inspired life begins to feel almost essential. We desire only to be in the flow of what feels good, we open willingly to that which resonates for us, we notice and we act upon only that which rings true for us. We become attuned to mis-alignment or mis-match and can swiftly re-direct our course. This does not mean we avoid challenges or calls to growth. When we are willing to be with 'what is', even when 'what is' is uncomfortable, we are offered a chance to discover our resistances and to discover what they have to teach us. As we get clearer in our truth we come to know the difference between flow and avoidance.

And when we really don't know, when we just cannot get clear on where we want to focus our energy or what we want to create, we have the choice to sit with 'don't know', to allow and accept the not-knowing. We can wait for inspiration to call as it surely will when we offer ourselves up to the silent mystery of life. With *Faith* and *Impeccability* by our side, at some time or another, we will know.

Experiences with Impeccability

Bathing in *Impeccability* was, for me, like a profound home-coming. It radiated a high and pure light that was utterly soft, divinely inspiring and quite magnificent. It connected me with a profound sense of commitment to myself and my journey. The soft lusciousness of the golden and blue-lilac oils put me into a space of such abundance that I could feel wealth, in all its myriad forms, enfolding me.

Melissie shares an initial experience with *Impeccability*:

When I bathed in Impeccability I saw my Dad and he was always the saintly easy parent, but I was suddenly so filled with anger that he was not there and I had to deal with huge abandonment from the male side. I also saw very clearly how I abandon myself by not claiming or using my masculine side. It is easy for me to be creative and intuitive but very hard to access the organisational skills and logical mathematical side. So with this bottle I worked very hard to be aware of the imbalance and to bring the two sides together.

The next time she bathed in this bottle it took her to a completely different level.

After Impeccability I can see with clarity that it is all impeccable anyway. We do not have to do a single other thing. God is impeccable and we are part of that so already perfect. The previous time I used this bottle I was worried about judgements coming up, but now I cannot even access the judgement. It is just perfect.

The comment I most often hear from those experiencing this Key, this bottle, is that they feel held. Its Divine Masculine energy offers a palpable depth of support. It's also becoming known as the Zen bottle. It puts us into an almost monastic state of peace, tranquillity and silence. It's also where we find the 'shoulds' and the 'musts' beginning to pack up and leave. There is simply no place for them any more. We find ourselves clearing our clutter – mental, emotional and physical – and allowing ourselves more space to breathe and to just be.

Impeccability reminded me that it is more important to have all the questions than all the answers. Being impeccable is to know who we are and to dare to ask as well as daring to envision what we are becoming. I feel humbled by this experience. It is so simple, power comes to us when we are ready to bow, when we are ready to step out of ourselves (our sense of individuality, ego) and ask Spirit. Then we are no longer small or big, we just are Divine. As the Divine, we call to us our dreams.

Claudia

What I really got is that for me, the masculine here is the structure, network, grid, clarity of BEing. If this is all illusion, then it's a virtual reality we have set up in order to "play the game" - we never meant to "suffer the game". We set it up because, as an illusion, it's perfectly safe to find the outcome of our beliefs and truths. Even if we 'die' in the attempt, we are immortal in original reality. Whatever we think or do, we cause no harm in reality, only virtual experiences that reflect our truths. So the old truth that Earth is a hard school falls away, and we have Earth as a safe, protected space into which to bring our reality of being while finding out what effect our 'truths' have on ourselves and all our fragmented selves.

Shelley

I am embracing all that this wonderful bottle is bringing to me. It's hard at times knowing that whatever challenges face me are of the reality I make for myself. This week has been a roller coaster ride for me - huge ups and downs - but the magical moments ..wow. I am exploring how my impeccability can help my light and love become receivable. I am understanding that however willing I am to live my light and give my love this does not mean it is easy for others to embrace. I am looking deeply into the mirror and trying to tune into the silence - with faith I know guidance will come. And more than ever I am loving the journey that has brought me to this point in my life. Through working with Impeccability I am discovering my authentic self in the depth of the silence.

Silvannah

Having been a "doing" person for most of my life, I am finding that that all I now want is to "be". Impeccability is almost forcing me into slowing right down. I can't wait to get home at night just to be still and quiet.

Christine

This bottle has really raised my awareness of when I am being impeccable and when "I am not". I literally hear a note of truth ringing in my ear when I am in total alignment and boy how I stutter over the words when I am not! I am so grateful to have had this time of reflection and feel empowered to take action when called to do so from now on. The other thing I got loud and clear was to live without judgement, attachment or any resistance at all. It feels great and so freeing.

Claire

Generosity

The Third Key: Generosity

You yourself, as much as anybody in the entire universe, deserve your love and affection.

~ Buddha

Gliding On Generosity

As I explore this Key I recognise that being generous with others is such open-hearted expansive joy. It also feels very generous to myself. I am consciously connecting with the joy vibration and it is rich, wonderful, liberating. Always enough, all ways enough. Yes, I know it to be true. I love connecting with the vibrancy and lushness of the *Generosity* bottle. It opens my heart and warms me every time I see it or think about it. I feel old uncertainties slipping away. Life takes on a more generous hue, colours are more vibrant, the space around me is more buoyant. I am very aware of giving to myself and the joy of receiving is a welcome embrace.

Generosity opens my heart space and offers me up to life and life comes rushing back to meet me, arms open wide. The more expanded and open I am the more generous my life becomes. I begin to breathe generosity, to feel it in my pores, to feel it beating inside my heart.

Generosity takes me deeply into gratitude and I find that appreciation and gratitude are inextricably linked with generosity, indeed they seem to me to be almost the same thing. As I allow appreciation for what I already have – money, fun, friendship, joy - to flow through me, more of it can show up. And it does. As my week with *Generosity* goes by noticeable evidence of it appears in my life. Abundance flows to me in all ways, proof if I needed it that what we focus on expands. A concentrated focus on generosity, abundance and receiving leads directly to experiences of those things in my life in even greater substance than before.

Generosity of spirit becomes my over-arching theme. In conversations with others I take more time to listen than to speak. I notice how paying for something can be joyous if I feel the generosity of the universe in making available to me the funds I need to pay for it. I can even enjoy a sense of generosity in the paying of a bill – it can feel like a gift, if I let it.

Sitting in my garden on summer days I am awed at the abundance and generosity of nature, spilling over with gifts of sustenance and beauty. All around me are examples of the universal flow of abundant giving and receiving.

I take some time, over my days with *Generosity*, to explore the connection with the feminine and what it means to be female. Whether man or woman, the ability to receive is a function of our inner female. She holds a receptive awareness that allows, opens and accepts. She is generous-hearted and as we open more to her, she offers us richness, warmth, love. *Generosity* takes us into relationship with our inner feminine, seeks out the places where we withdraw or withhold, and guides us gently into a more fluid and receptive space where giving and receiving become the joyous rhythm of life.

Generously Transforming

Thousands of candles can be lit from a single candle and the life of the candle will not be shortened.

~ Buddha

With this third Key we prepare ourselves, readying for the process that is to come. Transformation is no longer just a possibility. Our circuits are being re-wired, there is a quickening of pace and we begin to open to a deeper harmonic ebb. Drawn further into the gold, we discover that we are being activated and attuned to higher consciousness.

Expansion is a key-note of these coral-golden tones, opening us to the gifts we already have and to new ones of which we have yet to dream. Coral's ability to absorb shock means we can expand safely and gently without recourse to growing pains. We begin to expand easily and naturally in balance and in harmony with our true Divine essence.

Generosity draws us out of *Impeccability's* introspective space and invites us to dance with the world. It encourages, cajoles, nurtures us out of our cage. In a gentle paradox, it enables us to experience the fullness and richness of life whilst remaining empty, open and still.

Generosity takes the limits off. What might be possible? Everything!

Bottle G11: Generosity (Coral/Pale Gold)

The coral is unconditional self-acceptance – I am perfect as I am - and the pale gold is our connection to our authentic Divine selves. This combination very powerfully reconnects us to who we really are, Divine Creations – magnificent humans able to joyously dance our reality into being. If we are perfect and perfectly aligned with our Divine self we can create anything. This bottle is therefore all about harvest, abundance, love, joy and generosity. If we can finally see ourselves as a part of the Divine's perfection there is nothing we do not deserve and we can therefore access and generously share all of it. The love that we hold for our precious self is so attractive that it can attract anything and anyone we focus on because we are in alignment with God's truth for us. This bottle holds the "missing secret". This is the key to manifesting joyously.

The Golden Pathway

The path from *Faith* to *Impeccability* paves the way to step into *Generosity* and the true deep self-acceptance that is found in the colour coral. The Keys begin to show us in practice the Divine order and pattern that Melissie and I had recognised in them from the beginning.

As we relax into generosity, we discover that our faith has given us even more reasons to have faith. We discover that faith and generosity sit on the same energetic line. They are entwined and interconnected, the coral of *Generosity* being the complementary colour to the turquoise of *Faith*. When we are generous with ourselves it is, in part, because we have faith; faith that there is always more, that there is always enough, that we are always enough. When we are in faith, we open ourselves to the generous beneficence of the universe.

When we are in faith we discover a closer connection with our impeccability and when we embrace impeccability we learn how to be 'for' ourselves, to listen and to hear the notes of our soul. Generosity is the next step, naturally unfolding.

Harmonic Three: Generosity

In the cool, pale stillness of gold and blue-lilac you opened to the sacred space where you could claim your note and your voice. Now, in the honey-caramel tones of coral and gold, your note sounds out into the world and you begin to dance to your tune in joyous recognition. Your note goes out and joins with others to become the dance of life. Here you play your note. Here you play your tune. Here you play. You are in alignment. You are in harmony. You are in joy.

The generous notes of coral and gold call you to dance. Will you dance your talk? Will you dance your joy? Will you dance your life? You begin to notice how your note, your tune joins with those of others. Who do you choose to dance with? Whose note complements your own? What harmony can you, together, create?

The coral and gold of *Generosity* step you into your body and dissolve the fear-bonds you have created that have caused you to withhold. When you have withheld from yourself or another it was because you feared there was not enough. Held in the warm beating heart of generosity, you *know* there is always more.

Here you begin to claim your natural state and that state is abundant bliss. You are resonance and resonant, and you are called back to harvest, prosperousness, good fortune. You are more than enough and now you know it.

You claim and live your life as wealth, in wealth; as generosity, in generosity; as joy, in joy.

Rich, full-bodied and sensual, these colours are your password for perfect happiness. Together, they are a key to body bliss. Warm, full-hearted, buoyant and expansive, *Generosity* reminds you that enlightenment comes when you step over and beyond the belief that your body is the problem.

An enlightened body is exactly the point.

Ascension is taking your body with you.

Ascension in a body is perfect bliss.

In your body resides the hall of records that sits in your cells. Your records are calling to you now. The wisdom of all that is, lies hidden inside. Will you answer the call?

Coral is the colour that dances in the Christ ray. It summons the Christ consciousness within to shine forth onto the golden earth. Life on the new golden earth is luscious, precious and dazzling.

So too are you.

Living Christ consciousness on this planet is utterly sweet and divine and it comes when you give and receive unquantifiable love for yourself. It comes when you give to and receive from all. It comes when your joy and love emanate out into the cosmos, like a bell that is struck at exactly the perfect moment. In the light of your Christed self you know you are the beloved. You are the Divine acceptance of your magnificent self. You know and joyously receive your power, your light, the Divine truth of your body.

This is the quickening, the lifting of your vibration. Here you accelerate; here you give life to your truth, your note. You come to life, enliven, awaken to the potent generosity of your spirit, your mind, your body, your being.

Inspiration flows in, generously, abundantly, and you know which actions to take, and your actions are guided and flowing and seemingly without effort.

Pure rich abundance guides you gently into sweet simplicity. Feel the taste of it on your tongue. Feel its touch on your skin. Sigh. Breathe. Release.

Coral and gold ask you to be in joy, to live life. Their message: "Don't waste it!" Life is such a precious gift. Play. Enjoy. Be.

Ascension begins in joy. Ascension is the gift of a life lived in joy. Ascension and joy are two notes sounded together as one.

From out of the silent space, *Generosity* births the new.

This is inspired beingness. This is life *lived* on the new planet.

The true preparation for Ascension begins.

Keynotes of Generosity:

*   Expansion
*   Quickening
*   True self-acceptance
*   Giving
*   Receiving
*   Dancing
*   Play
*   Fun
*   Joy
*   Abundance
*   Wealth
*   Bliss

The Quickening

If there were only one gift I could give, a single reward you would value over all others, it would be this word, this experience, this Holy Offering that has the power to transform the whole world. Live within the YES!

~ James Twyman

Generosity takes us into a completely new space. It births us into a harmonious state of being that is unlike the previous two Keys yet perfectly prepared by them. We have delved deeply inside ourselves in the cool turquoise and blue-lilac and we are now ready to lift out and up into a gentle new day. The rays of sun-like *Generosity* warm our bodies and our spirits. We feel ourselves opening to them, expanding and reaching out. The pace begins to accelerate. Having immersed ourselves in the cool still silence we notice that we can now bring more of ourselves into the light. We are ready to engage, to connect, to share.

From the void space of *Impeccability* we discover that there is sound and light, movement and potential awaiting us. Inspiration strikes the open space and gently ignites us. We are preparing for action, for the dynamic expansion that has been incubating in the silence. Coral holds us steady in the light of unconditional love as we take our first tremulous steps.

Generosity Dances

In generosity we no longer focus solely on ourselves and our journey. We open our eyes and our hearts to experience the richness of life lived among others. We cannot discover our fullness in isolation. It is the interactions and interplay with others that shows us to ourselves: magnificent; flawed; perfect; human.

Generosity asks us to explore questions of relationship:

Who are we in relationship?

How are we in relationship?

How do we dance with life? Do we dance at all?

Do we enter into the tapestry that is woven by each step of the dance or do we remain on the periphery, unwilling or unable to become part of the unfolding design?

When we live generously we are willing to be fully present with another, to show up whole-heartedly in relationship. We offer ourselves in all our truth and we open to be with and share with and discover another. In generosity we are more interested in participating in the dance than in the perfection of the steps or the grace of the movements. We give of ourselves and we receive what others have to offer us. We dance. We play. We connect. We feel the gratitude of being a part of the dance. Sometimes we dance with heavy feet and little skill. At other times we amaze and delight ourselves with our dexterity and polish. It is not the talent or otherwise for dancing that concerns us. It is to be in the dance. It is to be the dance.

Generosity stops us from taking ourselves so very seriously and gifts us the ability to smile and even laugh at the extraordinary, complex, exquisite and intricate ride of life.

Generous Enough

The coral and gold tones of *Generosity* shed light on our beliefs about giving. When we withhold from others, whether it be love, money or time, it is often because we fear there is not enough for us. When we withhold we withdraw from others and also from ourselves. We shut down the giving and receiving channels from fear of lack or just plain fear. When we withhold we are in the opposite of faith.

Generosity stops us withholding. Generosity opens us to the gift of giving, to ourselves and to others. We *know* there is always more. When there is always more, we can be abundantly self-loving. As we give to ourselves first and foremost we find the resources which spring naturally from a place of abundance and we discover the joy of giving to others. In generosity we expand into the infinite wealth of the universe and, with robust faith, we live from that place. Giving generously to ourselves and others becomes a gift and a joy that is richer the more we engage in it.

There may be hard-wired beliefs to overcome. We may have been told that to give to ourselves is selfishness. "Putting others first" is a well-worn mantra we may have taken on at a very deep level. Yet if we refuse to give to ourselves, if we withhold from ourselves, our giving to others comes from a depleted cup. Without receiving we become dried up, squeezed out, washed up. When all our giving is to others, when we have not yet learned the art of receiving, we set up an imbalance within. We develop over-giving muscles and become a distorted version of ourselves, eventually burning out or burning up with resentment and frustration. Like a wheel that is out of balance we end up veering across the roads of our lives, unable to find any true direction and more often than not ending up right where we started.

Why might we be reluctant to receive, when the universe is so willing and ready to give to us? Might it be because we don't truly believe we deserve? Without genuine self-acceptance we might consider ourselves unworthy of the gifts available to us and be caught up in the deceptive web of "not enough". Not good enough; not loveable enough; not worthy; all the ego's falsehoods that negate our innate impeccable divinity.

Where do such misconceptions arise? Very often in childhood. And as we are asked now to give and to receive, wholly, unconditionally and divinely, our childish wounds are triggered and raised up to the surface to be seen, recognised, held, loved and released. Generosity asks us to give up these fictitious beliefs and open to the truth. What do we gain from holding on to these stories? They serve only to keep us bonded to the victim state, hostage to our worn-out myths. Generosity melts such bonds and warms our frozen child-hurts in the gentle glow of unconditionality.

True generosity gives and receives in equal measure. In generosity we flow and dance with others. Our wheel is oiled and balanced so that we can go in any direction we choose, open to the possibilities of the road ahead. Generosity is the opposite of martyrdom, sacrifice and over-giving. Generosity is not selflessness, it is self-full-ness, giving fully of ourselves and opening fully to receive.

Generosity is the opposite of fear and survival. To be held in the heart of generosity is to thrive, to blossom, richly experiencing all that is offered, sipping deeply of life's ever-replenished cup. As we nurture ourselves, gentle ourselves, caress and honour our beautiful selves, we step into another dimension entirely. *Generosity* offers us a portal to a higher vantage point, a more robust and engaged connection that transcends the petty, the mundane, the false. *Generosity* opens the gateway to true self-acceptance. When we can claim this, we can claim our I Amness, all the time.

Unconditionally Generous

Until we fully embrace generosity and the perfect cycle of giving and receiving we may find ourselves trying to control things in order to justify our behaviours or beliefs. Perhaps we find ourselves experiencing coral issues of getting attention through drama, illness or trauma rather than being authentic and open about our needs. Perhaps we hold back, limiting ourselves, restricting the flow of generosity in our lives, attempting to remain 'in control'.

Where is our generosity tempered by conditions?

Where do we put limits on what or how much we will give or receive?

What do we withhold from others and from ourselves?

Love? Money? Time? Knowledge? Our presence? Our true selves?

How do we do this? Why?

The generous combination of coral and gold offers us the possibility of knowing and accepting our divinity, our light, our power and truth. When we know this, we no longer need to be in control or to impose conditions on our giving or receiving. We come to see that letting go of control is the only path to authentic truth and power. When fear, doubt and lack of trust arise we may think we need to be in control, yet if we come back

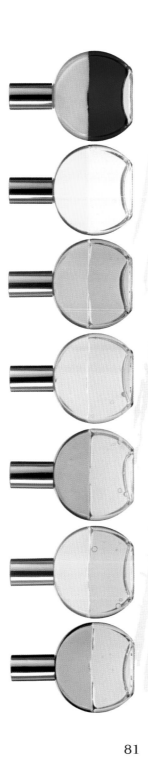

Golden Ascension Keys

Faith

Impeccability

Generosity

I AM

Grace

Ascension Light

Satori

Gold Angel

The Golden Keys and their accompanying Angel essences

to faith, we recognise control for what it is: an ego-tool and a profound disconnect from our authentic Divine selves. We are asked instead to return to *Faith*, its turquoise the complementary colour to the coral of *Generosity* - two sides of the same golden coin. When we come from a space of 'always enough', we are happy to give without condition.

As we visit and re-visit these colours, these themes, we see how they invite us time and again to give up the games, the stories, the justifications. They invite us into a relationship with ourselves and others that is true, authentic, clear and uncluttered. They invite us to wash clean our jaundiced eyes, to view through the eyes of the Divine and to unconditionally love, honour and accept firstly ourselves and then others.

Conscious Generosity

Though we may be delighted by the prospect of a life lived in generosity, our memories and conditioning sometimes send us warning bells. What if giving turns to over-giving? What if giving leads to being taken advantage of? What about the times we gave of ourselves and never, apparently, received anything in return? Many of us have become so unclear in our giving and receiving that our boundaries have become thoroughly blurred.

The foil to generosity is the ability to set healthy boundaries so that giving to others is balanced with a generous sense of self-worth and self-value. When we move into a space of conscious generosity we give and receive appropriately from a place of whole-hearted and unconditional love for ourselves and for others. Setting positive boundaries is foremost about being generous with ourselves. If we value and honour ourselves we give ourselves support and love and then find we are willing to both give and receive generously and – and here's the key - consciously.

Our interpretation of generosity defines how we experience it. On occasion it may be more generous not to give than to give unconsciously. In the Key of Impeccability we discover what it means to be impeccable with ourselves. In Generosity we learn to become impeccable with others as well as ourselves. Generosity only becomes an issue for us when we are not in impeccability. When we are impeccable and coming from pure inspiration rather than memory, our giving flows naturally, easily and without expectation. In impeccable generosity we have no need to hold on, to withdraw, to withhold. We can truly be in our abundance.

Impeccable generosity is both completely conscious and completely inherent in our divinity. Impeccability holds boundaries innately within it so that when we are in impeccable generosity we are in alignment and in integrity with ourselves. Giving then becomes a natural extension of who we are, not something we feel we should do. A 'should' is not an act of generosity and it is not impeccably aligned with our truth. When generosity becomes an inability to say no, we risk a slide into the murky waters of resentment, overwhelm or apparent victimhood. Our power is diminished. Our self-worth recedes. But in the golden generous light of conscious giving and receiving we can take back the flame of our ignited heart and cast off these slippery illusions. When we are in alignment with our truth we no longer need to over-give, to give without conscious awareness or care for self. We no longer attract the energy of 'taking'. We just dance the generous dance of the universe, giving and receiving freely and the more we give the more comes right back to us. Generosity reminds us that everything is within, that all our experiences are simply a mirror.

Generosity: Joy and Prosperity

Generosity takes us out of mean-spirited and shallow reservations and limitations into buoyant possibilities and potential. The richness of the coral and gold *Generosity* bottle takes us instantly to the possibility of joy and even bliss. Our open-hearted gratitude paves the way to further delight.

Generosity opens our hearts to wealth, abundance, prosperity; and that, after all, is where the abundant gifts of life will find us – in our hearts. We know that it is only when we resonate with something in the core of our beings, in our essential selves that it can flow easily and abundantly to us. We can attract through our thoughts, it is true. Yet when we engage our heart, really open its valves to the prosperity frequencies, we turn up the volume on our attracting abilities. Why? Because the heart is the seat of our true selves, the heart is where our soul rings out its Divine note. The heart is where our joy vibration resides. Joy and wealth are intimately linked. In joy we already feel wealthy and when we feel that wealth, we open to receive more of it, in all its myriad forms.

Generosity is the knowingness of our worth, our deserving, that resides deep in our heart chambers, allowing us to reach the fullness of our light. Golden-coral *Generosity* takes this knowing right inside the body. It washes out the lack and the beliefs of undeserving from the cells, depositing instead encoded messages of light, sound and colour, messages of unconditionality and love which the cells respond to and decode.

We start to understand that the body is not the enemy of our bliss, not the detractor from our Ascension process, but a key, a gift and an incredible guide along the way. Our body informs us, instructs us and signals to us. It gives us experiences that are the envy of angels and those who are beyond physical form. Ascension, in this earthly lifetime, can *only* happen in the body. Our body becomes our tool for enlightenment.

Divine Consciousness

Coral paves the way for us to explore our human divinity on Earth. It is the colour of the light and the depth of human form expanded into infinite oneness. It is the colour of that which we call Christ consciousness but which may also be named Buddha consciousness or enlightened consciousness or Divine Presence. The name is not so important. What matters is the energy it carries of pure awakened light. Contained within *Generosity's* gold and coral blessings is encoded information to remind us, at a cellular level, of the Divine perfection we all carry within. Christ consciousness is the awareness of the pure, impeccable and accessible light we hold that goes beyond judgement, beyond limitation, beyond the mind's imagining into the vast expansiveness of all that is. It is the offering of the Christed-ness within each one of us.

We are reminded of our soul's quest to be the truth, to be the light, to be in a suspended state of pure awareness that transcends ego and mind. Ascension is the attainment of this state whilst *in a human body*, something that has never yet been realised, until now. Christ consciousness is being offered, here, now, to all. It is not a blessing bestowed upon a chosen few. It is available to everyone. We are supporting and assisting each other as we travel, some a few steps ahead, some a little newer to the path, all in this together. Our combined willingness to journey into this sacred dance means it can happen that much more easily. The collective power of our spirits means that Ascension is not a dream or a delightful game – though it is also both those things – but a reality as solid and as 'real' as the third-dimensional one we have believed ourselves to exist in for so long.

Divine Feminine

As we explore generosity in all its many faces we discover that one of them belongs to the Divine Mother. She is the light and the expression of the feminine in her Divine perfection. She is the grace and love of the Universal Mother.

The coral in *Generosity* offers us softness, gentleness, ripeness and expansiveness. It opens a gateway to our feminine aspects, to universal female energy, to the awesome light and power of the Divine Feminine. She offers us her bounty, her beauty, her ever-available nurturance and guides us gently to do the same for ourselves. She takes us deep into our creativity and encourages and nurtures the fruits of our unfolding. She offers us her sweetness, but not the saccharine sheen of false promises. This is the full-bodied ripe deliciousness of universal joy.

Generosity asks us to meet the female within, to discover her stories and her beliefs, her talents and her fears. She asks us to connect with the female receptive strand of our beings, to open to her light and to explore what female means.

Where in our lives could we be mother to ourselves? Where could we open to sustenance, nourishment, plenty and prosperity? Could we ignite our own creative Divine spark and open to its richness, its gifts, its expansiveness? Could we meet our inner female and embrace her?

Generosity in Action: What Does Generosity Look Like?

What does it mean to be generous? How might generosity show up in our lives?

In some situations generosity may be about giving or receiving time or attention. In others it may be equated with material prosperity. In still others it may be a quality of character that cannot be measured or quantified but that emanates from us or to us. Generosity may mean giving without condition or expectation of receiving. It may be giving when we have little to give. It can be as simple as listening to someone in need or opening to their viewpoint without judgement. Generosity may mean we are fully present to the person we are with instead of mentally juggling a multitude of thoughts and only half attending to the other person. Generosity may mean giving for the sheer joy of giving. It can be giving ourselves the gift of time, space, freedom from worry or self-judgement. It can be having generous thoughts and sending love and abundance through our beingness.

We find that generosity is a choice like all the other Keys and that it can be cultivated in all its various facets. We may find ourselves reviewing our habitual thoughts around giving and receiving and developing a more generous approach to others in our daily lives. We may find ourselves noticing our heart energy more as we give more. We may find generosity itself leading us into the heart of interconnection with all and discovering that our essentially generous nature is only enhanced when we tear down barriers and open space inside for the gift of another's heart.

Generosity takes us to the warm resonant hearth of life where we gladly share our essence, our glorious true light. It is the boundless, joyful giving and receiving that comes so naturally when we are in alignment with ourselves and the infinite, ever-loving Divine.

Exercise: Living Generously

(1) As you connect with Generosity over the course of a week or more, play with giving to yourself each and every day. Give yourself something you value, treasure, delight in – time and space for yourself, creative pursuits, gifts which make your soul sing. What would it be like to commit to being generous to yourself?

(2) Take this opportunity to explore how it feels to give to others during this time, to give without question or validation or need. Explore your feelings about giving to others as you do so.

(3) Each time you pay for something experiment with opening to joy and freedom as you do; expressing your gratitude for the wherewithal to pay for what you need or want. Play with viewing money as an endless supply of energy that you can exchange freely, all the time.

Experiences with Generosity

The taste of freedom that comes from when you accept who you are, as a Divine creation, is one of those experiences to which words do not do justice. I chose to work with the Coral Angel and Gold Angel sprays alongside this bottle. They brought cleansing tears and a realisation that conditions are very much a man-made thing – we even set conditions on what we expect to receive. This bottle says "bring it on, it's all for you and me". I feel that I am seeing a set of scales and they are unbalanced. I like to give out, but am not always ready to receive. Why? Because I feel unworthy. As I am working with this lovely bottle, a lot of healing is coming in and I see an abundance of good things all around me. I am using a mantra "to me, through me, from me". Nothing is limited, only our perception. I can fulfil all of my soul's longings. Faith, trust and honesty are all coming in with this bottle.

Diane

I loved this bottle. The energy felt like being wrapped in pink candyfloss in the bath. It was very loving and nurturing. There was one strong message and that was that I should stop seeing everything as an ordeal to be survived and instead just enjoy each experience. I realised that I have not really been looking after myself as I should and that I must start giving myself some of the nurturing I give to everyone else. Money also came up with this bottle. I have known for some time that I have been undercharging and selling myself short, but have not had the courage to put my charges up. Halfway through using this bottle I found myself putting up my prices and having the confidence to do this.

Anne

My feelings of 'not enough' are disappearing like mist with the second round of Generosity. I have been waiting for this all my life.

Moira

Right away I found this bottle easy to do. People smiled a little sweeter, chatted a little more. When it came time to pour it into my bath I decided that I would keep in the spirit of the name, Generosity. So I filled my MP3 player with an abundance of good up-beat music, had a small buffet of chocolate and a pot full of water and ice to keep my drinks cold in my now hot steamy bathroom. I also felt a near uncontrollable urge to light some candles. My theme was abundance and joy; I wanted lots of the things I liked to go along with the usage of this bottle. As I lay there I made a conscious effort to focus on the good things in my life that I had and or wanted in abundance. Good times, good people, love, happiness, interesting, intelligent friends, inspiration and money.

I had been told that this was the female bottle as well so I spent some time committing to allow that aspect of myself to come more to the foreground. I'm not entirely sure I had much of a choice in the matter, but it makes me feel better to think so!

The next day I sat down at my computer, and wrote a sonnet and three book concepts in about two hours. Inspiration was leaking out of every pore, one great idea after the next. Happy to be writing again I didn't think too much of it until that night when I realised I had the concept but no actual story. So the creativity was there, but no direction to take it anywhere. And I thought that must be the heightened female aspect, a bubbling pot full of ideas but you need the balance of both male and female to do anything with it. It's not about dominance of one aspect of self; you need the balance to get the concept and the story. What's the use of a good idea when you don't do anything about it, and what's the point of just doing when you have no idea? Marriage suddenly made more sense to me, as humanity seeks outwardly the change they want in themselves, to bring together the male and female and marry them to have a greater understanding of the universe.

David

Generosity is asking me to be generous to myself, to be kind. It is giving me permission to bring out the feminine side of me which for years has been dominated by the masculine through circumstances (or so I thought and of course it didn't have to be that way). I find myself wanting to be protected and nurtured. I held Generosity to my heart last night and felt that it was helping to remove the barriers that have been "protecting" me from hurt (by the men in my life) and I now feel more open to receive the love that my heart seems to long for. I also felt that I was wrapped in a cloak of white feathers. I woke up several times last night, once with the words "transmutation process" resonating in my body.

Christine

I know now why I have such trouble in letting go and tipping my whole bottles in the bath at once. It's about being in the now. The bottles are showing me that in their beauty they are for now, at this moment, for the week and just because their physical glory has been tipped out into the bath the connection and messages can be accessed forever. There is no need to hold on physically to anything because replenishment is there but we have to let go for the new to come in.

Jo

What a shift to be able to forgive and love with every cell of my body. I just want to sing and dance and thank the universe.

Silvannah

A tale from Melissie:

I have a friend who takes meditative 'back to nature' hikes through the Karoo - which is the desert area just behind the Cape Mountains - and she always takes some of the angel sprays with her. This time a baboon came into her tent, took a bite out of a pack of angel cards and when she spotted him he dropped the cards and grabbed a bottle of Gold Angel under one arm, a bottle of Coral Angel under the other, and scarpered into the veld. Never to be seen again. Getting in touch with generosity, abundance and his female side no doubt.

I AM

The Fourth Key: I AM

If I AM love I can trust the universe to support me because the universe AM love too. Whatever we claim for ourselves is all we're ever going to see outside of ourselves, because we can only ever see through the eyes of what we are AMing in that moment. If I am miserable I will only see misery, if I am Divine I will see only the Divine.

~ Melissie Jolly

I Am Gold

As I connect with this Key I open to a world utterly dazzling, a world full of possibility where I know that all is available to me. I am taken into the heart of the sun, radiant and glorious. I am shown that I am this too. I find here a purity, simplicity and clarity of light such as I've not known before. Whenever I connect with the pure gold *"I AM"* bottle I feel streams of golden light reconnecting me to something greater, the evolutionary force of the cosmos.

As I hold it, the energy of this bottle is like a huge river swirling all around me. The promise and possibility this Key holds is so huge that it is both slightly scary and completely wonderful. I am in the moment, riding this swirling river and I am on the crest of another moment and another and another. With this golden power Key nothing can be tied down or fixed. It is fluid and changing and changeable. Gold swirls in me, through me, around me. *I AM* shows me that I can, indeed, create, and while this is a responsibility and a challenge, it is also pure delight and joy.

As I live in this fourth Key I am held in the heart of creative knowing.

I am everything.

I am nothing.

I am essence.

I am truth.

I am beyond thought and word.

I am earth. I am air. I am fire. I am water.

I am all that is.

I am that I am.

Bottle G12: I AM (Pale Gold/Pale Gold)

This is the I Am. When you choose this bottle you are ready to release all the beliefs that still say "I am not". When you choose this you are fully prepared to align with your Divine self and claim yourself as part of the Divine. The Creator and I are one. The Divine is within and I am that. Our addictions are the things that keep us small and keep us feeling separate from our Divine self. This bottle will support us in letting go of fear and the separating influence of addiction. When we claim back our true authentic power, we can be free of the addictions and be fearlessly, powerfully Divine.

I Am

One secures the gold of the spirit when he finds himself.

~ Claude M. Bristol

We are ready to embark on the next stage of our journey. We have gone within to find our faith, we have reached into silence to draw forth our note of impeccability and we have begun to experience the generosity that comes from sharing who we are. We have engaged with our maleness and connected with our femaleness and now, as we begin the fourth Key, I AM, we take on the mantle of our wholeness. We are poised at the mid-point on our journey through the Ascension Keys, carried this far on a golden wave of light. It is time to embrace our I Amness. But what does it mean: I AM?

The simple answer is that I AM is the name of God, the name of the Divine Presence in all. If we claim "I AM", we claim ourselves as God. To recall our I AM-ness is to remember ourselves as Divine. To offer up our I AM to the universe is to know we are beyond identity, beyond name, beyond appearance and beyond seeming "reality". I AM says just that: I am. Nothing more, nothing less. I am.

If we look deeply at what this means for our lives, what might we shed? Could we now release fear? Doubt? Worry? Judgement? The stories that have run our lives? Identification with names, labels, beliefs about ourselves? Could I AM be the key to finally setting ourselves free?

Harmonic Four: I AM

You have reached the pivotal point on your journey. There is now no chance of turning back, even should you wish to and you know that, in truth, you do not. You are curiously drawn forward in a natural resonant flow, seemingly without will and yet utterly clear that this is the pathway home.

As you walk into the wholeness and completion of pure gold, you come to know and understand who you are.

Here is where you begin to live your note, your tune. You resound with your note, you ring as your note. Your note emanates forth like a resounding golden gong. And your note is I AM that I AM that I AM that I AM, on and on, echoing into the infinite space of white-gold wisdom.

The alchemy of gold has wrought its magic and created a new being. You are the new being. You are the alchemy. You are the alchemist.

The creation of worlds is at your fingertips. You cradle them in the font of your love. This is your value now, creator. This, your worth. Inseparable from that which you would create, fashion, yield with the very marrow of your breast-bone. You are the creative force beyond reckoning. You are the tidal wave of love, ever-lasting.

Do you see now who you are? Do you see? Look closely. A tableau is being revealed.

There you are: shining your light, unmistakeably, unshakeably. You are. I AM. Your generous heart holds you graciously as you let go into the next harmonic wave and it carries you to shores unknown. You discover it has carried you home.

You are the creator, joyfully manifesting at every step. You move beyond old ways of living and being. You are; and what you are is all of creation. Now you live your light fearlessly, in joy, in love, in ceaseless creation. This is the shining light beyond all reckoning and you are that light.

The light grid around your body is re-aligned, re-connected, re-defined. You are infused with the gold I AM of your own Divine power. Liquid, fluid gold pours into your cells and your body is made of light. Your body rings with the truth. I AM all of this.

You are reconnected with yourself, reconnected with all, reconnected with the language of your soul, reconnected with the Language of Light.

You remember: I AM.

I AM calls you to be nothing less than the light you know yourself to be. With power comes responsibility. In the playful, abundant joy of *Generosity* you played God.

In *I AM*, you are God, and you know it.

I AM that I AM.

You are the expression of true, boundless, ultimate Divine power.

There is space now only for authenticity, power, light, truth. You know your value. You know your preciousness. You know your golden worth.

Now that you are this, you cannot slide back into the murky realms of limitation and separation. You can no longer be unseen. From here, your light simply is.

Love's pink tenderness is added to ego's strident yellow, turning it, melting it, into pure, heart - making gold. The ego is transcended.

As the gold touches you, really reaches you, deep inside your body, you understand and you know, with each of your cells' imprint, that love is the only power, the only truth.

The Ascension journey is no longer simply your personal calling to a higher place, a deeper space, an enlightened parenthesis. You are now on a journey to the golden heart of all that is.

Keynotes of I AM:

- Creation
- Alchemy
- Potential
- Possibility
- Identity
- Power
- Authenticity
- Wisdom
- Beingness
- Wealth

The "I AM" Key

In the centre of a figure of eight or lemniscate is the cross-over point where all things meet, the still point at the centre of the flowing movement of the infinity symbol. As we venture from gateway to gateway, from Key to Key, the golden *I AM* is that still point, the centre point where all things end and begin. It is the eye of the storm, it is a safe and welcoming haven. It is both a resting place after our travels and a portal to the heights we are about to scale.

I AM is at the hub of the alchemical process that is taking place within us as we explore this Ascension pathway. The golden *I AM* bottle is the alchemy of its component parts, the pink and yellow that mix so fluidly to create gold. Together they combine to create something that goes beyond all that they could offer individually. Pink and yellow are the colours of rebirth, renewal, re-creation and together they make up the gold of who we are now becoming. Gold subtly transmutes whatever is mis-aligned within us and combines with the potent force of our own light potential.

The secrets of gold lie deep within, often buried. I AM shines the light of consciousness into the depths of our innermost being and uncovers the treasure there. Each time we soothe and oil our bodies in the liquid gold of *I AM* we offer each cell of our body the light of its divinity.

I AM is the energy we emanate when we know our value and our preciousness and our worth and, in doing so, attract it back to ourselves.

I AM is where we face our fears and our addictions. It is the place we decide which of our stories of "I Am Not" we still need and which we are ready to discharge.

I AM is where we align with our soul's greater purpose and live the full and open truth of who 'I am' rather than a limited or distorted version of who we thought ourselves to be.

I AM is ho'oponopono*, the ancient Hawaiian technique for profound healing, transmutation and forgiveness which, roughly translated, means 'to set things right'. Ho'oponopono says we are one hundred percent responsible for everything in our reality - and that means *everything* - and that we can therefore 'clean' anything in our reality that does not serve us, that does not ring with the truth of our divinity. We have the power to change what we are creating in every moment through our thoughts and feelings. Ho'oponopono is a swift and powerful shortcut to creating what we want to create and to clearing memories or beliefs or conditioning that continue to create what we do not want.

The Golden Keys as a whole and the I AM in particular are in themselves a form of ho'oponopono. Golden *"I AM"* offers us 'cleaning' on a deep, cellular level. As we bathe in the golden glow of *I AM* we are literally cleaning out beliefs, thoughts and memories that no longer fit. Letting go of the stories that have bound themselves up inside our molecules. We are making space for the truth of our divinity to find its way into our bodies so that we can return to our essence and our light even while we inhabit them.

I AM gives us back the key to our power.

I AM is the creation of the new human. I AM brings together all the aspects of our being into a perfectly unified whole. Male and female unite in Divine harmony within us. Spirit and matter become two sides of the same magnificent golden coin. The elements harmonise and weave a magic dance in our being. Separation dissolves as we become one. I AM.

* Zero Limits by Joe Vitale offers detailed information on ho'oponopono; visit www.zerolimits.info

Who Am I?

The double impact of gold over gold really steps up the pace as we connect with the I AM bottle. We are asked to explore "Who am I?" "What am I?"

If we are to claim "I AM", what is it we are claiming?

Notice the power of I AM to manifest. If I say, "I am this", my reality serves to reflect that. If I believe "I am that", then it is so. We are called to notice our words, to notice how we speak to ourselves, to notice what we offer out to others. What are the undercurrents that flow to us beneath the waves of our words and thoughts?

The breath is our greatest doorway to the gifts of I AM. Each time we draw life into our bodies we have the opportunity to change the way we 'am'. Each inspiration carries infinite life and light and power. Are we willing to receive these blessed gifts? Or will we dampen the light, smother the power, chastise ourselves, chase the power away?

As always, we have a choice, in every breath, in every heart-beat, in every moment.

Who do we choose to be, here, now?

Golden Addictions

Gold is the colour that brings to the surface our addictions; our addictions to chaos, to control, to dramas and stories and battles and behaviours. Yet our addictions, faced with the potency of our golden I AM truth, are but tiny scared creatures, scurrying about, clamouring for attention. What if we were to love them as the teachers they are, fear-enslaved though they may be?

What really are our addictions? Are they keys in themselves? Guides to the places where we still hold on to small concepts, to powerless thoughts, to disempowered behaviours? Our addictions are our fears made manifest. We are addicted to control because we fear what will happen if we are not in control. We are addicted to drama because we fear what we might be required to look at in our lives if we did not have the drama. We are addicted to food or alcohol or cigarettes because we fear our bodies and our emotions. What are addictions if not the salve we use to smooth over the cracks in a fragile ego?

Our addictive behaviours and thoughts provide what we hope will be a panacea to our fears, keeping us feeling that we are actually in control of our lives. Usually these behaviours and thoughts and patterns end up controlling us. Addictions keep us locked on the wheel of separation, from life, from the Divine, from others. While we are in addiction we cannot be authentically who we are, who we 'am'. *"I AM"* - the bottle, the energy, the truth of this, is our key to uncovering where subtle addictions may be hiding in our lives. Chances are, we already know about our most obvious addictions. But are there others lurking in our closets? What would happen if we allowed this Key to unlock the doors and portals of our psyche? Might the frightened shadows emerge into its golden beam of love-light where they can find true resolution?

Golden authentic power is the opposite of addiction. Gold turns should into could, must into may. Gold liberates us from control and the bindings that have held us fast in the strait-jackets of our own design. As we step out of the grip of our addictions we allow the true glorious colours of our beingness to reveal themselves. We allow our I AM to shine forth.

We begin to live our I Amness. We begin to claim our I AM.

Family Gold

As we connect with this Key the colour gold invites us to notice our family issues or conflicts. We are called to explore issues of money or power in our family, to winkle out and recognise patterns and threads that run through our genetic line. Where are we blindly falling in with family beliefs about money or lack of it, perhaps following behaviours set up by our parents or previous generations? Are there questions of right – the right to be ourselves; the right to be heard; right versus 'wrong' ways of being or living; the right to family money or power? Perhaps we are engaged in family power plays that keep us from being authentically who we are.

Whatever patterns we find woven into our family tapestry we can be sure we will be acting at least some of them out on the wider stage of our lives. Family patterning goes deep – into the very DNA – and it takes a courageous and un-blinkered commitment on our part to discern, acknowledge and shift them. Golden *I AM* shows us the patterns, lights them up for us to see. It then offers us choices. We can continue to follow these old familiar paths, swallowing down and suppressing the innate knowing of our truths, or we can take a beam of golden light and slice through them, revealing the impeccable golden light at our core.

Authentic Gold

Be yourself, everyone else is already taken.   ~ Oscar Wilde

This Key opens the gateway that leads to our authentic power, the power that belongs to our own sense of truth and beingness. But what makes true gold? What makes us authentic?

Whether it is in family or other relationships, our sense of who we are is often tested and tried. Part of the value of relationships is in their offering of a testing ground for our beliefs and behaviours, to temper us as gold is tempered by fire. As we journey through life we will at times be forged by our experiences, at other times melted by them. Perhaps we will allow forces to shape us until we become clear about the shape we would make of ourselves, for we can only create ourselves out of total self-responsibility. When we claim the I AM we discover we can wholly create ourselves and our experiences in every moment. We have that power. Once we are imbued with our authentic I AM, we can create who we are with the dance of our life in every moment. We discover the sound we make, the colours we are, the pitch and frequency of our unique tone. We find the channels and avenues that will support our unfolding beingness. We discover what resonates for us and what does not.

102

We discover that being of service is a core component of life, something that makes life purposeful and meaningful. When we stand in our true power we are inherently of service to ourselves and others, simply by being authentically who we are. As we claim our I Am we move out of servitude and into service.

When we listen to the golden voice of our heart, follow the golden thread of our essence, feel the golden light of our soul, we become authentic. We speak from a place of truth – our truth, not that of another. We act from a point of resonance within us. We see from a higher viewpoint, one that is not clouded by limits or judgements. We find our impeccability and we live from it. Our masks and layers of falsehood are stripped away leaving only our essence, our brilliant, beautiful, awe-inspiring light. In authenticity, our note rings out with perfect crystalline clarity and is heard across the cosmos.

Golden Heart Power

I AM is the Key of power. With this Key, if we choose to, we can remember the power that transcends worldly control and open to a realm unimaginable from within the limiting confines of the third dimension. In this greater expanded space we find the true power. The power that is only, knows only, gives only love. The heart is where our true power resides. The heart is the force-field of life, the pathway to love, the power-house of infinite oneness that takes us beyond the ego's need for dominance or separation.

What would happen if we reclaimed the heart-power of solid gold that knows itself as Divine? What choices would we make from a place of empowerment about our life, our work, our play, our life design? In so doing, what responses might we elicit from others? Whose buttons might we press in our new, empowered light?

In I AM we become aware of patterns of ego power emerging or being brought to the surface for resolution. We discover the places we have withdrawn or given away our power to others. We remember the times we have used our power to manipulate or control. What we now realise is that this was a distorted power, a power that came from ego, a pretended power arising from fear, a false power offered by the limited self. Our glorious I AM offers these patterns up to us so that we might find the blessings they contain and release them.

When we claim I AM we can no longer hide from our truth, our light and our authentic sense of self as an empowered Divine being. If I AM, and

I AM truth, I AM gold, I AM light, I AM Divine, how can I possibly deny my ability as creator? How can I possibly be a victim?

And what does that mean? To be unable to blame, shame or judge another? If I AM Divine, if we are Divine, we are also responsible, fully and utterly, for our responses to life, our choices, our paths, our creations. All of it. This gives us true power - the power to create, fully, our own reality. It frees us to release everyone that we have perceived as 'out there' to the infinite whole, the inter-connected oneness we already are.

I AM, You AM, We AM

If "I AM", then you 'am' too. In I AM we take whole-hearted, whole-souled responsibility for our thoughts, our actions, for all that shows up in our lives. We see the perfection in all. We know that each time we say 'you' we are speaking of an aspect of 'me'. We know that each time we criticise, judge, blame, gossip about or deride another we are simply bumping up against an aspect of them that is a mirror of what is inside us.

When we know that all is Divine, all is whole and perfect, we are freed from the ever-present desire to control the lives of others, to 'rescue' or inflict our apparently greater wisdom upon them. When our antennae are attuned to the searing, ringing inner sounds of our truth we know when a word, an action, a touch is required and when it is merely the posturing of our ego-selves, the small needy niggling aspects of ourselves that feel duty-bound to control, manipulate or direct. The great news is that the 'we' we have become accustomed to thinking of ourselves as, is not now and has never been in control! The moment we release into a greater, higher, broader, deeper, far more expansive vision of ourselves we align with our truth and anything we do or say simply becomes divinity experiencing itself.

I AM is the return to oneness, the remembrance of our soul-fuelled journey. It is the coming together of our apparent polarities, the integration of our assumed duality. I AM is the return to the whole of which we believed we were only a part. I AM is divinity in action. I AM is night becoming day and the understanding that it was only ever thus. In I AM we begin to claim our God-realisation, our self-realisation and to experience the Divine in all things and in all ways.

Everything 'outside' of ourselves now becomes us. We are the I AM.

Golden Wealth

This is the wealth of spirit that cannot be denied. In the richness of I AM we radiate a light and a warmth and a magnetism that is immediately attractive to all that we would create. Wealth is not so much something that comes to us, it is who we are. Gold is the frequency of wealth. This is wealth which includes and yet goes beyond material abundance. It is the all-encompassing wealth of beingness that emanates from us and to us as we recognise our worth. It is the wealth reflected by treasure, jewels, diamonds and yet it surpasses them in its value. It is the wealth we embrace when we awaken to a life fully lived in the truth of our own Divine light.

Creator Gold

We are creators. It is *our* universe, our life.

In the Key of I AM we become manifestations of light waves and sound waves and thought forms of gentle knowingness.

In I AM we plant those seeds of knowingness in the soil of the new golden earth and we watch in awe as new life bursts forth, infinitely unfolding before our very eyes. It is unstoppable, this creator force.

I AM shows us who we are, Divine manifestations of that creative force, the light brought to Earth; the creator and the created.

In I AM the creative power of the galaxy intersects with the life force of our essence. We burn a trail across lifetimes leaving only light. We are transitory. We are eternal.

Nothing can remain as it was. Nothing is left untouched. We are taken into a wave of evanescent light and asked to doubt nothing. We are drawn into a flash of brilliance which even as we enter it begins to disappear as we fold in on ourselves, returning to the allness we have become. We are turning for home.

Light waves align themselves with our newly opened eyes. Patterns dance and collide, exploding in Divine configurations of light and sound as we return to Source.

We are the sound of the universe, the in-breath of the tide on the shore, the out-breath a subsidence to our natural form.

We are love, always and only.

Meditation: I AM Breath

Find a quiet place to be. Hold your bottle of golden I AM in your hands or place it wherever you feel drawn to on your body. Begin to follow the rhythm of your breath. Notice the in-breath and the out-breath without trying to change anything. Feel the sensations in your body as you breathe. Allow yourself to sink into your breath, letting it carry you on its ebb and flow.

Begin now to notice the possibility inherent in each in-breath. Each one a gift, an offering, a blessing. Notice too, how you have the choice of how to respond. You can accept or refuse, embrace or deny. But it comes, nonetheless. And the next. And the next.

As you open to the possibilities, the choices, the life inside each breath, begin to repeat to yourself "I AM" with each in-breath. Let your I Amness unfold as you repeat this mantra. Let it reveal you to yourself.

When it feels appropriate, begin to draw gold into your being as you breathe in, allowing it to flow into your body while repeating "I AM". Continue for as long as you wish.

When you are ready, allow your breath to carry you back to your surroundings and to the present moment.

I AM in Action: What Does I AM Look Like?

Think for a moment of anyone you truly admire, someone who stands out for you as a luminary, a shining light. What is it about them that draws your admiration? Their words? Their actions? The way they look? Their success? Whatever it is, you can be sure they shine the light of their I AMness brightly. If you take a moment to really consider what it is you are drawn to in them, you may find it is a subtle glow, a quality of energy that emanates from them, no matter what they do or say. More than likely, they too have human 'flaws'. Very probably, they are not saints. Yet they are so truly themselves, so unafraid of their light, so unashamedly in their beingness that they emit a high-vibrational frequency that touches others in profound and meaningful ways.

One such person I know is a woman in her eighties who has lived a thorough and inspired life. Always a pioneer she has forged trails wherever she has travelled. She owns an unshakeable sense of worth and an open-hearted willingness to grow right until she takes her last breath. She does not shy from the trials and challenges of life and she gives of herself endlessly. Yet she also knows the value of giving generously to herself and offers herself the same care and appreciation she offers others. She gives and receives love. Quite simply, she is love, the ultimate expression of I AM.

Experiences with I AM

With this golden I Am, there is the opportunity for the deepest cleaning. It felt as if it was physically flowing into my liver and clearing lifetimes worth of anger. It also brought up the opportunity to clear some very specific past life stuff and it brought some surprisingly clear seeing. I normally sense angels but after this bottle I can see them. As I was bathing in the I AM oil, suddenly there was this craggy old man with a cowboy hat and drawling Kentucky accent and HUGE golden wings. He came and sat on the side of the bath and when I got uncomfortable about being naked he said "I can only see your light, Ma'am." Very polite. And then there were just waves and waves and waves of golden light.

Melissie

I went into meditation with I AM. I placed the bottle on my heart chakra and felt immediate peace, expansion, golden pure light flowing into my heart. I felt my heart expand with loving energy, golden hearts flowing out in abundance into the universe. I felt such Divine, pure love. So sacred. I felt so joyful and loving, peaceful and golden! I went for a mindful walk and began to really relax and reflect the true I Amness into the space. I stopped in the middle of a huge field and felt the expansiveness of my energy field and the love for everything around me. A little later I stopped, closed my eyes, arms outstretched and connected on a really deep level with nature. I felt such deep peace and joy, gratitude and love for being here today. I began to understand that what was around me in that moment was all there is and to surrender in to the moment.

Claire

I have known and accepted for some time that I create my own reality. I now realise why I feel so different - my acceptance of creating my life was in my head but I AM created a shift in perception for me - I now know in my heart! That's why I feel so good and it makes creating my daily experiences so different.

Tabora

I felt a particular attraction for this bottle from the moment it arrived. When displayed, it has a wonderful auric glow around the top fraction of the bottle. I felt that it would be an important bottle for me to work with.

107

Within the following 24 hours we experienced yet another dramatic change to our family circumstances. We have been left high and dry again. I turned to my bottle. What would it teach me, what would it help to release? The answer came quietly, but in a profound way.

If we are to really embrace the concept of "I am" it has to be felt in the heart. We can think the "I am" and talk about it, but it only holds truth and a foundation, when it is experienced for real within the heart. The heart will not be fooled and always knows our truths. So the I AM bottle has become my heart bottle. I have made friends with the financial problems we are beset by, and still have peace in my heart.

Diane

And so we all spiral upwards, ever evolving, ever ascending. With each turn I seem to bump into an old version of myself and am once again reminded of who I am not. Those are the tough times because those are my addictions. Yet with each turn upwards it is also a little easier, a little less dramatic. So often we hold onto those old selves, being creatures of habit. It is in a sense easier to be the one who is a drug addict or the one who cannot cope with life or the one who is sickly, or the one with no money. These are the things that we have used in the past to define ourselves but this is not who we are. Those experiences were necessary when they were necessary but there comes a time when they need to be released if we are to ascend and not get stuck on the spiral. Those old selves need to be explored, understood, felt and released. The essence of who we are awaits us. Fear needs to be released. Faith needs to take hold in our hearts. Layers need to be peeled off so that we can find our true authentic selves, our true power, our golden light inside. What is this fear that we give so much of ourselves to? Fear of what has happened in the past when we did let our light shine? Fear of abusing the power that we have as we did in the past? It has become a comfort zone, a conditioning. But it is not who we truly are. We are not fear. We are not small. We are larger than life, ever expanding, ever brightening. We are creators and explorers. We are the essence of God. There is no limit to light. Once there is light we can see all. Let us look closely at what we put in front of us, the mirrors that arise in our lives and the messages that the Universe brings. Let us examine these things and take with us only that which we need. Let us release the stuff that no longer serves us on this spiral of life. We are allowed to be who we really are. When we realise that nothing bad ever happens then it becomes easier to take the risk of believing in our truth and if we follow our truth then we can release the old stuff and move up the spiral and in so doing, create new experiences and a new world. A heaven on earth.

Nicky

Grace

The Fifth Key: Grace

Give up to grace. The ocean takes care of each wave till it gets to shore.

~ Rumi

Grace-Full

As I begin a week with the Key of Grace I find myself drawn to read the words of the "Harmonic" out loud. The only one here to hear is my elder statesman cat who totally zones out as I read, soaking up every molecule of grace as it floats to him, carried on my voice. Afterwards, sitting in stillness and silence, I feel a strong shift taking place in my crown and my body. I reconnect with an elder, a Maori woman, a woman of ancient wisdom and knowledge. She is part of me, she is me. She knows and sees and is utterly connected with the land, the earth, the universe. She is as old as time. I like her, very much. She guides me gently, softly, to mother myself. She shows me that I am my own mother, that I have the power to birth myself every day, every moment.

Spending time in the company of the pink and gold *Grace* energy takes me into a fluid space of such light, serenity and quiet stillness that I lose the desire to 'do' anything much at all. I experience a time of comparative solitude, where though I feel the inter-connectedness of all, I gift myself this time just for me. In grace I discover more of me – the illusions and the truths - through the reflections others graciously show me. I find unconscious defence mechanisms which had been submerged coming up for air, giving me the opportunity to see them for what they are and to dissolve them in the grace-filled light of acceptance and love.

As I walk in grace's golden-pink flush the colours around me are softer, the light gentler. Time slows. I feel the notes of a bird song like harp-strings, like heart-strings. Flowers radiate their brilliance and beauty. Trees hold out their energy fields to me and ask me to be still and feel what it is to be *this* connected to Heaven and to Earth.

Shimmering light surrounds everything I see.

Bottle G13: Grace (Pale Gold/Pale Pink)

This delicate colour combination is there to remind us again that only love exists and that everything we have experienced was chosen by us as an expression of Divine love. Here we step into grace and we forgive ourselves. We were never guilty, we were Divine expressions experiencing. And nothing was ever not part of the plan. These colours indicate a rebirth but this time without the trauma of death. We gently rebirth into our true selves and remember that the Divine is love and that we are that too and the true power that creates everything is love, love, love. This is the female face of Divinity and it is beautiful and so are you. While using this bottle it will serve you to take time every day to remember something fabulous about you. If you write it down you will make it that much more real. Take time to honour your female creative intuitive vision.

What is Grace?

Your task is not to seek for love, but merely to seek and find all the barriers within yourself that you have built against it.

~ Rumi

Grace is a subtle quality of resonance that defies the relative clumsiness of words. It is an energy to be felt, to be heard, to be experienced, to be lived. It is a frequency modulated to perfect peace and enlightened beingness. It carries an exquisite tenderness in its rays.

Grace is a blessing to be showered upon ourselves. A beneficent, shining stream of light to be poured lovingly through our veins. It is a fountain of pure radiance, divinity declaring itself our most stalwart supporter.

Grace is pure love. In its light the unlovable becomes loved. The unacceptable, the ugly, the wounded within us, all are embraced in the feather-light touch of grace. The unforgivable becomes love experiencing itself. The one we could not forgive – whether ourselves or another - is bathed in the holy fragrance of Divine absolution.

Grace is gifted, never earned. Grace cannot be worked for or achieved. It is fulsomely given, without hesitation, without limits and without condition. This is the love of angels.

In the pink and gold of Grace we let go of the past, erase it, opening to a new beginning, a rebirth. The past becomes just another moment. We cease to even recognise its former hold on us. We step out of pre-conceived thoughts and ideas and let each moment reveal itself. Grace takes us out of time.

Grace guides us to surrender up those places we remain stuck, our blocks and congestions. The warmth of grace dissolves the sticky solvents of memory, belief, conditioning. The most tender, most whole-hearted expressions of love melt the rigid structures of our self-imposed limitations. In grace, we know that the true power is love and we know that love is who we are.

112

The colour pink connects us with hearing, with sound, with music. In grace we begin to hear not just our note, our tune, our song, but a whole choir, a heavenly angelic choir that attunes us to the love we are in essence. Grace connects us with the harmonic overtones that sit above our core note and reverberate on and up into the silent planes of existence. It is sound beyond hearing, the sound of love, of the cosmos. Grace takes us above the noise of our mind and the braying of our ego and elevates us to a higher harmonic resonance. Grace gifts us the song of our soul.

Harmonic Five: Grace

In the pink is the hearing and the heard. The hearing and the heart. The heartbeat of your sound. Your sound rings out and it is the sound of love that creates universes. Creation reverberates to the sound of love and moves from the formless into being.

This is the harmony of the spheres, the galaxies, everything that exists. This is the music of the universe, the sound of the universe, and that sound is love, and that sound is you.

The cosmic sound of love rings out.

You surrender into grace.

This is where you finally understand, in the totality of your being, that the Divine is standing beside you, within you and before you and has done so all along, offering you to yourself, offering you to grace.

You claim it all and surrender into the love that knows no bounds.

You glide on a pearl-pale sea of grace that takes you beyond deserving, into the warm-hearted welcoming of love.

In grace you are benevolence, graciousness, benediction. In grace you are Divinely given, Divinely received. In grace, love is given and received without favour or question. In grace you are amplified love.

Subtle gold combined with delicate pink and infused with love, form the coral jewel that is the Christ consciousness, the true state of grace. Feel how the shifting light of golden pink gifts you with the utter claiming of your Christed, given, grace.

All things become blessed.

All things become blessing.

You are the blessed. You are the beloved.

Here, in grace, you bless, sanctify, glorify, exalt and magnify all on your path.

The note you have heard on your journey, the note that has lighted your way, is now integrated in your heart. You are the note of your heart, and you live it.

This is grace.

An angel's wings brush your face. A messenger imparts wisdom and confers light upon you. You heed the call and you respond.

All the aspects of your soul's greatness that have split or splintered from your being now return. You receive them and receive yourself, reintegrating and realigning with your wholeness. In grace you open to your magnificence and receive it. You are brought into communion, into unity, into wholeness. All aligns within you as One.

Where once you blocked love, damned up its flow, all becomes clear to you now. You are gifted the possibility of knowing yourself as love, of releasing that which has stoppered you, shunted you, stunted you. You are the open vessel and you receive, with grace.

The way becomes clear. The dam is unleashed. The road beckons.

And who will you meet on your travels?

Follow where grace leads. Follow her into the heart of Divine Love.

Follow her to You.

The love of the gentlest mother gifts you the rebirth of yourself to yourself.

In grace you birth your magnificence, soft and bright, and it summons a host of angels. The light is all you can see. Love is all you can know.

All that is, is the Divine made manifest in every form. All that you see is yours. Seeing the world through divinity's rose-coloured eyes, you are shown the new world you have birthed, the world that always was and always will be.

Grace is yours.

Grace is eternal.

Grace is the name of freedom.

Keynotes of Grace:

- Love
- Blessing
- Innocence
- Surrender
- Releasing the past
- Rebirth
- Harmony
- Beauty
- Gentleness
- Nurturing
- Simplicity
- Freedom

Rebirthed in Grace

Everything becomes new. All is re-born into a fresh new start, a brand new heart, free from the taints of fear, doubt and judgement. There were no mistakes. Nothing was ever 'wrong', least of all us. We move beyond forgiveness into the knowledge of the ever-unfolding perfection that is and that we are.

In grace we begin to acknowledge ourselves as love. We undergo a transformation of the self. We experience rebirth, renewal, returning to life, returning to love. In grace, as in generosity, we are deeply connected with the energy of the female. We become mother and daughter; Divine mother, Divine child. We move beyond identification with gender altogether or any concept of female we may have held. Grace speaks to us with the creative voice of the cosmos, the intuitive and subtle inter-weavings of light that would show us the truth of ourselves.

As we connect with this Key we are asked to be exquisitely gentle with ourselves, to honour and revere the Divine life of which we are manifestations. Being reborn into grace gives us the unique gift of gentling, nurturing and blessing our very own new-born selves. Grace takes us out of the cycle of blame and shame into the light of jubilant open-hearted celebration of the oneness we know ourselves to be. We begin to radiate from our essence selves, no longer closing off our brilliance. We remove the stopper and the wondrous glow of our light is revealed.

115

Surrendering to Grace

Grace allows us the experience of surrendering into our hearts. To surrender is to give up needing to 'know' with our heads so that our hearts might lead us to truly know. In grace we offer up the fragmented frightened aspects of our being which seek to be safe, to be in control. We loosen our moorings and float free of the limiting cords of that which our minds would tell us is power or control. We let the waves of grace-light carry us and find that we are utterly held and loved. We surrender further still and discover that it is we who are holding and loving ourselves, gift-wrapped in the tender warmth of our own sacred Divine heart.

As we surrender, beliefs, patterns and conditions we once held onto become nebulous. Goal-posts shift. New awareness arises. We become the observer of our unfolding present even as we live it. Our perspectives change. We notice what was once hidden from view, clouded by our misty pre-conceptions. We see through the eyes of love and all becomes clear. Surrender brings long-awaited freedom.

Grace gently shows us where we still hold limiting beliefs or thoughts that would prevent us from aligning with our Divine truth. We are shown where we continue to believe in 'outside' versus 'within'. Grace takes us to the place where we recognise that the issues we hold with another are simply our own, reflected back to us so that we might see, recognise and understand them. Grace gently offers us the courage to face them – our issues, our fears, our beliefs - and stand before them in Divine wholeness before offering them up to the All. We slip into the quiet existential space of home, full of grace, free.

I Am Grace

In Generosity we stepped into acceptance of ourselves in all our flawed perfection. In the golden glory of I AM we stood firm, tall and glorious in our I Amness. In Grace, we pivot, pirouette, spiral, dance into full-hearted, wondrous love for ourselves.

Grace invites us to fall in love with ourselves. To open to ourselves as we would a soulmate. To love ourselves as would a mother. To be with ourselves as would the truest friend. We are asked to bring love into every fibre of our being. The energy of grace takes us deep into the love of our utterly naked selves. It takes us from the self-acceptance of generosity into the genuine warmth of purest self-love.

Having claimed our I AMness we are now offered the opportunity to embrace the totality of who we are, should we choose to. Once again, the Keys offer us choice. Grace is freely given. Will we open to receive it?

When we open our hearts to grace all that was splintered off from our wholeness, all that was separated through fear or shame or trauma has space now to return, enveloped in the loving arms of our grace-filled selves. Grace is opposite of dis-grace, the opposite of shame and blame. In grace we are innocent. In grace we move beyond forgiveness. There is no need to forgive because there is nothing to forgive. We are shown in Grace's transformational light that guilt does not exist. Here, the illusion of guilt can be relinquished, offered up, transmuted. Without fear, without shame, without longing for that which we are not, we are free to receive that which we are. We become receptors for everything that is available to us from the loving grace that is in all. We open to the vastness of our innate beauty and behold the delight that is everywhere before us.

We discover the harmony that is inherent in all things, in the universe itself. We know ourselves to be an intrinsic part of that harmony, inseparable from the endlessly renewing, ever-weaving web of life. Time becomes irrelevant; past and future disappear. The holographic nature of life re-asserts itself as we become aware of our presence on altogether brighter, higher, clearer dimensions, offering us the power to transform. We attune to the frequencies our soul would show us. We see through the lens of timelessness. We know ourselves to be beyond all that time and space would reveal. We are duality made into one. We are the formless and the form. We are the presence that releases the past.

We step into grace and surrender who we thought we were and receive in the process who we really are. We are both the blessed and the blessing that we would bestow.

Grace is ever-present.

117

Meditation: Being the Blessing

Breathe in the energy of Grace as you hold the bottle. Feel gold and pink light fill and surround you as you become grace. Begin to focus on the energy of blessing and allow it to flow to others. Let the energy of grace, of blessing, emanate out from you.

You may be aware of specific places or people or situations you wish to bless or you may like to just allow the blessings to flow to wherever they are called.

Spend some time here and allow the blessings to well up within you and unfold before you.

Begin to be aware that as you offer blessings up, simultaneously blessings come back to you. Notice all the blessings you are offered. Receive them all.

The more you bless, the more blessed you are. Feel the fountain of blessings that flow to you and from you.

You come to realise that you are the blessing. Each time you breathe out, you offer a blessing. As you walk the planet, you are a blessing. You being you is the blessing.

Let the energy of grace take you where it will.

When you feel complete, come gently back to your surroundings.

Grace in Action: What Does Grace Look Like?

When we are grace we shine with a gentle radiating power. It is a quality we embody rather than anything we say or do, though it also penetrates our actions and our words. In grace we exude an energy that is both magnetic and accessible. Our worth is undeniable, as is our beauty. Love spills from our pores. We know that we are Divine, all is Divine. Grace comes when we simply are. It is not sought after, not bestowed on merit, not a gift given to the chosen few. It is the essence of who we are and we hold it in our cells, in our being, from where it radiates out to others. When we see and acknowledge the light of grace in others, we activate that light still further in them. When others see the light of grace in us, we become an amplification of that light.

The author Marianne Williamson comes immediately to mind as I contemplate those who emanate grace. Her words are messengers of light, her books are blessings in themselves. She shines with a transparent beauty and projects her spirit into all that she does. Another is the teacher and guide Samadarshini of the Oneness University in India. For me, to be in her presence is to know grace. She blesses and is a blessing simply by her beingness. You will know others who, for you, embody grace. As you consider this quality of grace, allow them to come to you. Let the energy of their grace radiate out to you and feel it connect with the grace within you. Notice how they are one and the same, that in seeing it in another, you also hold it within you.

As the spirit of grace blossoms within us, we rise to a higher dimensional space from where our grace shines out in all its magnificence. We feel grace within. We see grace in all. We are alight with grace. We are grace.

Experiences with Grace

I am so utterly in Grace and having a wonderful time. I feel as if I am being cushioned and nurtured. So much love coming from every direction.

Christine

It showed me how strong I am, who I am, how at peace I feel now, how calm I am now.

Carmen

It felt like I was bathing in a sunset - so beautiful. This week has been all about taking things very quietly and giving myself space to be. The message I have is "be gentle with yourself."

Shelley

When I first saw it I knew that I had some resistance to this bottle. It has turned out to be a huge one for me. I came to see the need to finally release my addiction to suffering and the need to forgive myself for everything this addiction has led me to do in the past. The need to understand that this was all a necessary part of my path and that the recriminations and negativity I feel in respect of all that have no place at all. I don't need to be ill any more.

Anne

The power and depth of this wonderful glowing harmonic is too immense to measure. It is taking me into places I couldn't have imagined. Discharging a maelstrom of uncomfortable emotion: anger, annoyance, frustration, grief, sadness, much lack of nurture (mostly directed at self). Your heavenly words for Grace touch such a deep place right inside the core of my heart. Bathing in Grace this morning with all the Keys and Angels and flowers I realise how the biggest rejection and critic through my life has been me. The heart-stopping words "I rejected all MOTHER LOVE" rang out to my being. I always held my true self back for fear of more outward rejection and of my own love for little Jo, choosing to place her in the critical place of "you are never good enough", enabling all I met to reflect and mirror that back to me. I give thanks and blessings to the magnificence of nature and the flowers I ran to for comfort which I suppose deep down I knew reflected my true colours. I have always felt behind bars, looking in on a garden of exceptional beauty and have been unable to reach the unutterable joy and love I knew was on offer, remaining somewhat serious and apart. I truly feel that these heavenly key harmonics have broken through the self-constructed barriers of separation and I can at last let my soul begin to shine out in true glory.

Jo

Ascension Light

The Sixth Key: Ascension Light

And then the day came,
when the risk
to remain tight
in a bud
was more painful
than the risk
it took
to blossom

~ Anais Nin

I Am The Ascension Light

I am light. I am Divine power. I am the Ascension Light.

During the magical week in South Africa when the Golden Gaia bottles are born, *Ascension Light,* of them all, calls me the most, its gold and white beauty reaching deep into my bones, my cells, the heart of me. Yet when it is time to bathe in its distilled light, I find myself in a state of fear, ungrounded and disconnected. Perhaps I know instinctively something of what this potent light will ask me to reveal. Perhaps, as has been said many times before, it is our power, our light of which we are most afraid.

When finally I take my courage and my body into the golden-white bath, all I feel is relief. Suddenly, it is simple. Ascension, I am told, is just the next step. Let go. Trust. All is perfect.

Afterwards, I am pole-axed, unable to do anything but lie down. I surrender to a humming, pulsating sound and light show that continues unabated for two hours. As it draws to a close, I hear the word 'exaltation'. I see my hands in prayer position moving upwards towards my head and then, in a gust of pink, white and golden light, hands open towards me. Light pours through. I am bathed in blessings.

I have an image of a wedding, all frothy white lace and dusky pink rose petals and glistening golden sunlight. I am offered the serenity, the light and the exquisite joy of a perfect new marriage. I envision bridal white, the palest of pink rose petals, joy, harmonious communion – a coming together of the male and female. This is a marriage not of two beings but of all that is within me. A Divine Union of the soul. The Ascension Light shines to me and through me in equal measure.

Ascension Light is a downloader, a reconfigurer, a re-wirer. I feel myself lifting higher, lighter, clearer each time I connect with it. I am transfused with the Language of Light, in my cells, in my core, in my essence. My body becomes swirling patterns of light. I see love wherever I go. I surrender into knowing.

Bottle G14: Ascension Light (Pale Gold/Clear)

The intensification of the light in this bottle lights up everything and with these colours you can also shine your light this brightly. It is crystal clear and this clarity will attract all the new crystalline beings that are incarnating now. They are here to show us how ascension works. Ascension happens when we remember that we are a light body, that we are the Creator's light in physical form and that the density we perceive in our reality is the illusion. This bottle will shine its light on everything that is illusionary and when the light is shone on the illusion it instantly dissipates. What we are left with then is the light of truth that is beyond illusion. With this bottle your cells begin to speak the language of light. Ascension.

Harmonic Six – Ascension Light

The sound of your light begins to ring on all levels of creation. Your cells attune to this sound, the joyous song of love.

Your cells begin to speak and to sing and to dance to the joyous harmony of all creation as you embrace and remember the language of your soul, the Language of Light.

The white-gold of Ascension Light is an experience of totality, solidified light, the light made real. It is you become whole, it is you become one. It is the reading of your soul map, the coming together of the territories and continents of your being.

Ascension Light is the amplifier of all you are and all you have perceived yourself not to be. Let it shine its light with the purity of knowing and feel its waves of energy peeling back the layers that have clouded your face from the sun. Its cleansing light ignites the flame of your truth and burns off all that is false within you. It welcomes you to re-define yourself as the light you have always been.

Ascension Light shows you that your seemingly solid physical body is simply dancing particles of light. As you speak, express and live the Language of Light you know that your body is made of light, the light of all creation made real in physicality.

The gold and white Language of Light rings this truth to the very core of your sacred bones. You hold the light in your physical body, like the awakened or enlightened ones. All that is not light falls away in the light of your beingness. The inaccessible becomes accessible. The truth becomes real.

Here you claim: I know and I am the knowing.

The Language of Light uplifts you to the next level. Your Ascension is in process. It is simply another step, one you know and understand at your deepest core and your highest height.

You cannot seek it with your mind. It is beyond all that you would imagine or believe.

Open your hands and heart outwards to the universe and watch in awe as the Ascension Light opens toward you and the light pours through.

With joyous clarity step off the edge of the world you have believed in into the transcendent, the sublime, the new.

You are become the Language of Light. You exist in the lightest, clearest space. You deftly dance into joy. There is nothing here but beingness.

In the gold and white you are the light and you are the creator of the golden age of transcendence. As you live your light, the golden truth naturally unfurls from within the fronds of your divinity. Enlightenment is not something that comes to you. You become it. You are it.

You reach this space when all the layers that have been masked and hidden by memories and responses and actions and conditions have been stripped away and underneath is the clear ringing tone of truth. To reach this space you have claimed I am faith and truth; I am impeccability and inspiration; I am generosity and joy, I am love, I am grace. I AM.

Now you claim: I am the light. I am the Ascension Light.

When you walk and speak the Ascension Light around the magical, mystical lines of the new golden earth, you activate the crystalline lattice of light that interpenetrates the newly forming planet. You activate the light lines as you walk; your being on the earth changes the earth. You are residing on a new planet and you are creating it with your every footstep, your every thought, your every breath.

Gold and silver step you into the angelic realms where the Tree of Life is encircled with the scintillating brilliance of your light. Exaltation is yours. The wisdom of angels is available to you now. They watch and delight in the vision of splendour that you are. You have walked the path and remembered the Language of Light and now you are there alongside them, with the journey in place and the information, the knowledge, the wisdom.

Let there be recognition within you of your perfect human design. Let the twin gold and silver lights of your authentic self forge a generous pathway home.

And yet, the journey does not end here. If your journey were to end now, you would no longer be here. Claim the light, become it, and then you can *be* it HERE, now, embodied.

Take the final step. You are home free.

Keynotes of Ascension Light:

- Pure light
- Clarity
- Harmonious communion
- Knowing
- Activation
- Angelic light
- Transparency
- Divine union
- Freedom

Creation Light

In the attitude of silence the soul finds the path in a clearer light, and what is elusive and deceptive resolves itself into crystal clearness.

~ Gandhi

In grace, we surrendered. Now we wonder, from surrender, where to from here? The answer comes: Into openness, into oneness, into wholeness, into freedom. All possibilities exist.

If we let it, this Key will take us swiftly and powerfully into a review of all that makes us who we have thought ourselves to be. If we let it, it will strip from us the layers of falsehood that have swaddled us and in its brilliant creative purity, recreate our perfect Divine blueprint. Here we begin to *know* who we are: the light of the Divine, housed temporarily in a wondrous formation of cells and tissue and bone.

The clarity of *Ascension Light* brings us into coherent alignment with our truth. This Key pulls back the last remaining layers of who we are not to reveal who, in essence, we are. New light rays are activated within us as we transcend the need for rules, for roles, for identification with this or that. As we let go of the need for anything to look or be or feel a certain way, we move into a clear, white space of endless opportunity, limitless potential. Here is the perfect blank canvas waiting to be drawn upon, a Divine blank template in each and every moment.

We move beyond trust into knowing and this knowing is a ringing coming from deep within our core. As it bubbles lightly to the surface of our consciousness we remember: we have always known this, always known our light. In the fullness of our knowing, we recognise now that all our needs are always met. There is nothing left to fear. Our spirit becomes free to alchemise our lives.

Ascension Light is a cosmic light-bringer, a creation crystal to assist us in shaping and patterning and designing the unfolding of our lives. Within its crystalline purity we are free to create anything we desire to experience. Unseen patterns form themselves in our light grids, scintillating points of light merge, form and re-form in each moment. Our intentions, our thoughts, our focus and our wandering wonderings create networks of light that reach out and connect with those of others. Our souls and hearts light up stellar pathways that guide us richly into kaleidoscopic bursts of evanescent love. We discover that they merge and come together when we open from our hearts, when we speak the white-gold language of love-light and when we ring the ecstatic chimes of our soul's call. Love is the language we have always known, deep, deep within. Love is the light we are. Ascension is our return to love.

Clear Light

The cleansing of the *Ascension Light* energy is felt by all who connect with it. A waterfall of pure light, pure love, pure essence is showered upon us. We are raised, lifted up, gliding on light. We are taken into the heart of the gold and silver sun-starlight.

As we reach a place of utter authenticity we acknowledge and recognise that we are the light and we are also the dark. All that we have perceived as our darkness, our shadow, is offered up to the grace of our light and we find there the truth that we are all of it – the light and the dark, the human and the spirit, of heaven and of earth; and all of it – *all* of it - is Divine.

As black represents the void, so too does the clear-white light. They are each the stepping-off points into the vastness of our souls. We have been through the darkness and we are the light and it is from the void that all light springs. We are the light that creates the Golden Age on the new golden earth.

The Ascension Light is a beacon, showing us the way home, preparing for us a pathway of light to follow, even as we create our own pathway in every moment that we choose to return to love. Each time we release fear or anger, each time we let go of resentment, each time we drop a story, a falsehood, a pretence, we are lighting the lamps of our Ascension path. Each time we step out of the little self and view the world from the height and breadth of our divinity, another lamp is lit.

Ascension Light assists us in clearing and illuminating our sub-conscious, but easily, without trauma, without drama, chaos or stress. The gold and white of *Ascension Light* smoothes, oils, eases the pathway home. We come to understand that Ascension is not something to be achieved, not a result of endless trying or doing but that it is effortless, an engaging of our soul's energy that carries us gently, easily, swiftly back to love.

In the gold and white rays of *Ascension Light* we find our innate purity, the purity of beingness that is inherent to our very existence. We find here a transparency, an openness of heart that enables us to see with piercing clarity who we are, who we are not.

In the light of our Ascension, in our return to love, we become illumined.

Ascension Language

In Ascension Light we begin to remember and to speak the Language of Light, the language our cells have always known but which we have allowed ourselves to forget. Why would we forget something so fundamental to who we are? For the sheer joy of the game? For the incredible gift of remembering? For the awe-filled ride of returning to our light? All of this and more. We are returning to the love that lies encoded in our very cellular matrix. Knowing it to be our essence, we risked to travel into realms of un-knowing. What might we discover about ourselves on the journey? Blinded to our light, what could we experience as one who is the light but does not yet know it? Returning home from our forays into worlds unknown, what new knowledge could we now bring?

With eyes open wide and hearts even wider, we find the language we thought we had lost. The Language of Light is the language of love and it rings louder than sound. Indefinable, unquantifiable, inexhaustible, love's tone is the basis of all life. The language our cells now begin to speak is no longer that of words, of solid 'reality' or logic. We open to new perceptions, we see from the lofty mountain view of Divine perspective, we call to us only that which is in resonance with our new fluid state of being. We speak without words. We hear with our hearts. We open to frequencies of light and sound known only to our souls. The high harmonic overtones of our soul's light ignite the path of our expression and shine through us, as us, from us. We pause now a moment and listen. If we listen with the soul's ear we will hear what it is our heart speaks of and knows so perfectly. All is life. All is love. All is One.

Divine Union

The energy of union permeates the Ascension Light key. We gather together all the parts of the generous mix that make up a life and begin to see where and how they fit. Communion comes when we let go of all we would hold onto and open to all that is already there, held resonant within us. Divine union is the ecstatic coming together of our body, heart, soul and mind into one sacred flame of pure light. In Ascension Light, we re-discover our union with all that is.

Sacred geometrical patterns and shapes show us the interconnection of all life, all universes and galaxies. We are each sparks of the one creative light, each of us lighting up the next light and the next, the interstellar grid of light growing every day through the magnificence of our collective soul's potent force. As we each light the beacons of our truth, the Ascension Light grows and spreads wings across the galaxy. We become one with Source and one with each other. Ascension cannot be a game of solitaire. We join and co-mingle our multi-coloured lights and create an illumination of spirit, wondrous to behold.

Activating the Ascension Light

Beyond time, beyond space and beyond form, our Ascension Light shines unerringly. Guiding us as we rise above the limits we have ascribed to ourselves, it echoes out into a bright new day. We are dying to the old, while reclaiming our right to live. We slip from the tangles and knots of memory into the gentle, gleaming light of Now. As we watch our old selves relinquishing their hold we are lifted gently and sweetly into life and find that it is richer, easier, ever more graceful. There is kindness and wonder to be found in its mysterious patterns.

We are taken into the unknown and the unknowable and shown the truth of life. We are gifted pattern and order within the dancing luxuriance of freedom. We are shown shifting light, fluid weavings, subtle connections. We surrender into the ever-knowing love of our heart's wisdom. We no longer seek to find the 'truth' or the answer for we know there is none to find. Only this: light; fluid and formless, generous and gilded, expansive and brilliant, ever changing and inextinguishable.

Our third eye acts as the transmitter and receiver of cosmic wisdom and energy, activated by the brilliance and clarity of Ascension Light. Spiralling light enters at the pineal portal and takes us into dimensional shifts, frequency modulation. Gateways to dimensions previously unseen, realms unheard, worlds unknown, all become available to us. Our all-seeing eye becomes the catalyst, the transformer, the transducer.

We stand on the brink of ever-lasting joy.

Ascension Light-Being Template Activation

Lie down on a comfortable surface, making sure that you will be undisturbed for as long as you need to complete this activation. For each person this time will vary, and could be anything from ten minutes to an hour or more.

Place the Ascension Light bottle on your high heart chakra (approximately the middle of your chest, around the area of your thymus). You may like to open your arms out a little, with palms facing upwards. Let your body be your guide as you receive the activation. If it needs to move, let it.

Focus your breath on the area of your high heart, where the bottle lies. Feel as your heart draws in gold and silver threads of light. Allow your heart to fill with these dual rays until it feels expanded, open and strong.

Begin to see or feel or sense gold and silver light rays beaming out from your high heart centre into the rest of your being, your physical body and your energy fields.

Watch as these light rays form a grid, a template, a matrix, all around your being. Watch as they spread throughout the template, activating, opening the channels of light within you, repairing the gridlines that have become damaged or disconnected during your human journey.

Allow the gold and silver rays to re-activate your Divine blueprint.

Feel the liquid gold and silver rippling through your matrices.

Your Ascension Light-Being Template is being activated.

You may sense or feel subtle shifts in your energy bodies, physical sensations in your body and emotional releases or expression. Allow them. Do not suppress or dismiss your experiences. Soften into them. Become one with them. Merge with the greater consciousness as you awaken to your Divine light.

Begin to sense your en-lightened DNA helixes spiralling about the length of your body, see them lit up with the light of your encoded blueprint.

Allow the activation to flow until it feels it has naturally finished.

Afterwards you may need to sleep, or you may feel very energised. Allow your experience to be whatever it is.

Ascension Light in Action:

Experiences with Ascension Light

I had to go and lie down after connecting with this one and it was like nothing I've experienced before. The only way I can describe it is multi-dimensional. I was experiencing myself in different dimensions at the same time.

Eleanor

The energy was extremely light in the bath and I could almost feel my body lightening under the influence. I didn't notice any other things until the weekend when I was doing a fair with a colour presentation and colour readings. I am an experienced speaker, but I still get the apprehension buzz before the performance which I could do without. However, this weekend I didn't have any of it. Instead I just had the realisation that I was finally the person I was born to be, instead of holding myself in reserve because of fear and resistance to who I am.

Anne

I bathed in the Ascension Light bottle last night, with three sprays each of Gold Angel and Clear Angel. Whilst lying in the bath I decided to do the Ascension Light-Being Template activation. I felt that it was easier for me to draw the gold and silver energies in whilst I was actually submerged in them via the oil/water mix. Instant result - I pictured my heart centre as a big gold and silver orb, with the Gold Angel on one side, and the Clear Angel on the other holding the orb between them. Lots and lots of high-pitched tones sounded in my ears which I know were angelic downloads. I now feel like I'm walking around with a big gold and silver helium filled balloon tied to me with a silver cord, and on the balloon it says: Caution - Ascension in Progress!!

Karen

The first time I did Ascension Light I had come through a tremendous cleansing time. In summary, Faith connected me to my contracts I made before incarnating. Impeccability was my incredible connection to the concept that there is only one and everything else is a fragment of that. Generosity cut me wide open surgically, cutting away everything I had ever used to define myself. I AM sewed me back together with a golden thread. Grace was a convalescence, where I had to be very gentle with myself and give myself time and love.

Ascension Light was where all the new fell into place. I was given my business name - Colour Connections - and from that, enormous changes happened and the networking began. Out of nowhere all was different and ever since my messages have all been about reconnecting with every aspect of my life and cleaning it up. Doors have opened onto old friendships that had somehow been broken off. Old hurts and problems have been exposed in love so that it is very easy for me to reconnect. I was given the idea to start a blog which networks in its own way, empowering and enabling others. All that I know is to be shared with others. My work with Colour Mirrors and special needs children has reached new dimensions. Ascension Light this time has highlighted the reconnecting and led me further down the road with the new children being born on this planet. The work I will be doing with these kids is so huge that every now and then I have to put everything aside and just walk - just to let it settle. Everything is so different. My heart chakra has been opened in a way I could not have believed - I genuinely often want to hug the person walking past me!

Shelley

Satori

The Seventh Key: Satori

Early morning, the orange sun is slowly rising, shining forth in empty luminous clarity. The mind and the sky are one, the sun is rising in the vast space of primordial awareness, and there is just this. Yasutani Roshi once said, speaking of satori, that it was the most precious realization in the world, because all the great philosophers had tried to understand ultimate reality but had failed to do so, yet with satori or awakening all of your deepest questions are finally answered: it's just this.

~ *Ken Wilber*

Satori Bliss

Satin magenta. Silken gold. My body thinks it has gone to heaven as I steep myself in the shimmery *Satori*-infused waters. I am shown a magenta planet where all the knowledge and wisdom of the universe resides and I am gifted with the knowing that all is available, nothing is hidden if we would but see. I am taken into the golden sun and deeper, beyond the sun into the pure golden light of existence. I become that light. I awaken to myself as that light. I am satori.

I experience a gratitude so profound that it shakes the very foundations of all I thought I knew. Waves of gratitude encompass my body; for my body, for this life I have chosen, for all those I've encountered on my path, for my teachers and companions in all their many forms.

This is satori. This is bliss.

I see myself being lifted up high, higher and higher still and I see that everything is exactly the same as it always was and yet it is utterly, wondrously transformed. I see more and with greater clarity now. *My* eyes have been opened, a gear-shift has taken place in my heart. I experience a huge gold and magenta ring of light going deep into my solar plexus, opening and expanding out to the truth and the magnificence of my freedom. I feel myself literally raised up as waves of bliss pour over me. I feel, see and hear angelic presences, the Christ light, ascended beings, but not 'out there' somewhere – right here, right now, with me and within me.

Afterwards, my whole body fizzes and sparkles inside and my cells take on a new vibration, a new note. Each of my chakras fills with gold and magenta light and I feel how it is to live this energy and light in each of them. My energy bodies take on this new vibrational frequency as it flows into my mental and emotional programs and responses. Here, we can release it all. Anything and everything can be transcended. It is, and we are, and all is possible.

Bottle G15: Satori (Solid Gold/Magenta)

This bottle makes our connection with our Divine selves a solid reality. It now no longer floats above us as a thought or a wish. It settles the truth into our cells that we are Divine and that we are living heaven on earth in this moment. This is the moment when we remember that we never left home in the first place and that heaven is where we are and that everything we see is Divine. It was never not that. This is the state of Satori.

Satori Is

Satori is a glimpse of the ultimate. ~ Osho

So, fellow travellers, we have journeyed far and seen much and grappled and wondered and revelled and realised and we are now on the pathway home. But were we not always so? Did we ever leave the sacredness of our innermost being? Could we have? What then awaits us as we unlock this final gateway with our seventh Golden Key?

The answer lies firmly in our own hands. We will see, experience and come to know exactly that which lies within our hearts. In satori we claim the knowingness of our Divine creative power to be and to experience. It is, as ever, our choice. We may view it as a completion, an arrival, an achievement. We may experience it as a full circle, a homecoming, a remembrance. We may understand it as a zero point from which everything emerges and to which everything returns. We may open the door to an enchanted garden of delight. We may turn the page of life's manuscript and discover all the wisdom, all the knowledge, all that is, written indelibly in our soul's light before us. We may ignite the fire of our heart and prepare to let it blaze a path of truth.

We may sense, understand, believe, may, in fact, come to *know* - at the deepest level of our being - that we simply are; that everything simply is. And it is in our body that we come to know this. Our body holds the keys that our mind would own but cannot. Our body united with our soul becomes the answer we have sought. We embody the light of our sacred fullness and watch as it transcends the need for anything else at all.

Harmonic Seven: Satori

When you are fully, utterly, one hundred percent yourself, you are no longer there.

The 'you' that you thought and believed yourself to be is gone. All that remains is the You that the Divine always knew you to be. You now know it for yourself. Outside of mind, thought or action comes the purity and clarity of soul-spirit connection to all that is.

Your frame of reference shifts. The world tilts on its axis. With a sunburst of starlit love, your reality changes. You awaken to a new light. The universe's window is thrown open. The sweet fragrance of life enters. An infinite second is split and the light of all knowing touches your soul.

Satori.

Unlimited bliss. Infinite space. The Awakening.

Aum is the sound of creation, amplified and simplified and accessible, brought into physical form. The Aum is satori. The Aum is your body. The Aum is you.

You are earthed, connected and grounded in the full-blown, resonant reverberation of the universe. Your note merges with the symphony of the cosmos.

Your magenta soul star is the microcosm of the greater existence. Each individual soul star aligns with and connects into the greater magenta soundscape of divinity.

Take this sound deep within your being and experience what it is to live this energy and light in each moment. Watch as it transforms and transcends any remaining patterns, programmes and responses. Offer them up. You are limit-free and untroubled. Your breath is the very breath of life itself, engaging, connecting, transforming.

Raise your light to a higher plane of awareness and see the expanded viewpoint of the limitless. All that you see is exactly what you once saw and yet utterly transformed.

Satori is the view from God's table. Satori is the all-encompassing vastness of I AM that you are. You live heaven on earth. You see beyond judgement. You know yourself to be without limits.

Here you discover your unique, individual, light expression of the Divine.

You are the allness, the glorious absolute AM. You are rich and luscious and reverberating; ringing, singing, emanating; and all that is, is Divine light. Enter gently this new space where your divinity reaches out to greet you and all that you see before you is encompassed in the glow of your own infinite light. You are the glory, you are the joy, you are the magnificence of ultimate surrender.

You reach into the light and discover there a profound thankfulness for this body, this assemblage of bone and muscle and tissue and life-force. You ring with the utter joy of this transient experience of earthly life. Ripples of gratitude and sparks of bliss appear on every level and are yours for the taking.

You sound your note and it is exactly the note with which you began the journey, attuned now to the very highest frequency. Your note has ascended an octave. Your note now is amplified and it reverberates through the waves of sound and light to become a Divine embodiment of rapture. You are bliss and definitive golden joy. The Earth lights up with your presence.

I am Divine light and I am that HERE, on the new golden earth.

I am at zero.

I claim my mastery. I am the master.

I am Divine.

I am replete with the song of life.

Keynotes of Satori:

- Awakening
- Breakthrough
- Perspective shift
- Transformation
- Gratitude
- Acceptance
- Integration
- Living our divinity
- Beingness
- Aum
- Mastery
- Knowing
- Home
- Sacredness
- Interconnection
- Beyond separation
- Perfection
- Oneness
- Unlimited bliss

Breakthrough

Satori shatters the illusions that have been clouding our view. It takes us above and transcends the limits we have set for ourselves. It literally breaks through our self-conceived barriers and enables us to remember and to know our wholeness. Satori often comes as a sudden awakening, a blast of light between our eyes, a thunderbolt of Divine timing. It is a glimpse, a flash, a keyhole into the heart of God. It may come as a momentary thing, an instance so perfect and impeccably timed that it takes our breath. It is not something we can control or hold onto. Rather it is the glorious package that we are given to unwrap when we let go of all need to control, when we surrender into grace and dive, without hesitation, into the awaiting moment, in the instant it arises.

Satori comes as insight, flashes of brilliance, Divine inspiration, swift awakening, instant transformation. We see what was before us but hidden. We view with piercing clarity what was obscured. We hear the heart-beat of our own Divine soul in its exquisite living rhythm. We travel beyond our senses into the realm of knowing and the world is never quite the same again. In satori, we do not discover that we can fly, rather we remember that we always could. Realisation comes, understanding dawns. In the emergence of our true selves we receive at first gentle touches of light, then stronger pulses of love then, as we evolve ever further, we are transported into full, resonant knowing.

Our perspective shifts. Light glances off a concept and transforms it into something quite other than what we thought we knew. Often, it comes when we least expect it, when our defences have crumbled. Our pulse picks up a different beat. Our hearts and minds are blown open. We tumble down the rabbit-hole into a waiting, awakening world.

Integration

We often have moments of inspiration or breakthroughs or "state experiences" when we see the world in a new, revolutionary way. Those experiences are, of course, awesome. And... they're only really meaningful if, after the initial buzz wears off, we have the discipline and the diligence and the patience and the persistence (and playfulness!) to create the structures in our lives that enable that breakthrough to stabilize and integrate and become a new way of being.

~ Brian Johnson

When the light of awakening strikes us, in whatever form it takes, we find ourselves on the threshold of a new world view, looking out over the horizon with wonder, awe, excitement, perhaps even with trepidation. Sands shift under our feet and we can no longer reference what we once thought we knew as solid foundation. At the table of delicious possibilities laid out before us we may find ourselves slightly bewildered, wondering which delectable morsel to taste first. Satori or breakthrough experiences are exquisite gifts which, even so, may take some time for our psyche to adjust to and accept. We may get high on the bliss of a newly awakened moment then find ourselves wondering how this can become part of our existing life.

Integration happens when we apply what we have learned to our daily lives. It also really only happens when we get out of our own way.

In the period following an insight, an awakening, a deeply penetrated truth, we turn to our souls to allow all the bright shiny new pieces to come together and form an integrated whole. *Satori* solidifies, amplifies and consolidates our spiritual nirvana experiences into real, present, accessible life. Were we to float evermore on the heavenly light rays of existence without anchoring them here in our bodies, here on the earth, we would live only half-lives. Our Ascension journey is a journey to the heart of all that is; all that is real, all that is illusion. It is the meeting-place of soul and body. Integration happens when we downshift the spiritual light of love and make it a solid reality in our homes, our hearts, our everyday lives. As the light of our infinite beingness radiates into every corner of our daily world, we become satori embodied.

Coming Home

The gold has travelled us along a routeway, a path to light and we are now reaching an ending and a beginning. We are moving up, ascending, raising our light vibrations and we are exactly where we always were. There is nowhere for us to go. We are coming home to ourselves. In satori we discover and uncover our unique, individual light expression of the Divine. As we recognise our own divinity, we see it clearly in others. We become aware of the greater weave of our individual lights and the interconnections that our lights make, each with each other. The network of light expands and grows stronger with each step that we take on the path back to ourselves. As our true authentic light reveals itself our own unique crystalline grid connects and joins and weaves with the work of the cosmic artist. Awareness lights us up and illuminates all. We watch in awe as we see ourselves reflected in the universe's golden mirror. We begin to know and to live our worth and our value and it is pure gold, solid gold.

We are coming home.

Return to Bliss

All of life is bliss. We seek it in the events, the happenings of our lives, when it is simply in the living that we find it. Bliss is in the everyday, the small moments. Life is. Bliss is. All the moments that make up a life are filled with the bliss of creation, if we would but receive it. Life itself is bliss. It is in the living that we experience satori. We are molecules, atoms, pin-points of exquisite bliss. If we are life and we are love then all is bliss, always.

We are shown glimpses of the infinite glory of life when we fall in love, give birth, transcend a fear, discover and follow our heart's calling. Yet the real return to our fundamental nature of love, of bliss, lies in the living of each moment of our lives, eyes open, heart engaged, spirit connected. There is not one experience or situation or second of our lives that does not contain the seed of satori, of awakening, of the possibility of enlightenment.

Satori, in its elegant, regal, magnificence, is a key to the moment. Magenta is the colour of now, its rich tones a melody of timelessness.

141

Interwoven with gold, it catapults us beyond ordinary, beyond mundane, beyond limited third-dimensional density into the explosive awakening of diamond light. It is a prism held up to our world-weary eyes that takes us into the very source of life itself.

Mastery

Satori is the gateway to mastery. In satori we become the masters we always were. As we reclaim our innate, Divine mastery we experience a truth more potent than any story we would tell about ourselves. Anything that is not in alignment with our greatest light begins to dissolve, to disappear, to slide back into the illusory waters from where it came. When we no longer need it to exist, it ceases to be. In mastery we 'need' nothing. All our perceived requirements are always met and we do not need to know how, when or where they might come to us. When we see a higher truth a lower truth no longer fits. Rising above what appears to be shows us what is.

In satori we know that time and timing always arise and unfold in perfection. We relinquish controlling and planning and even doing. Our footsteps are guided and guides, each moment an absolute expression of our creative mastery.

We sound the note of Aum. We dive into the sacred tone of all life and we emerge as infinite expressions of the one light, utterly unique, utterly conjoined.

Interconnected

A new structure is forming. It is the golden earth emerging even as we divine who we are. The new earth is constantly being created, just as we are. As we source our own light and reconnect with it we light up the field around the new planet. We are forces of Divine alignment. We create a cosmic weave, we ignite a universal web. We are united in wonderment at our own extra-ordinary and completely ordinary brilliance. We all join together in a meeting of whole-souled reverence.

Interconnections form between previously isolated structures. A plenitude of light lines is restored to the network of our planetary grid. The concentric energy lines that encircle our beloved planet intersect with the pure crystalline resonances of our chakric centres and form an explosion of cosmic energy. We are luminous, we are rain-light, we are dancing atoms of creative force. We cannot be undone. We can no longer be disjoined. We are one and coherent and whole. We are perfect Divine accord.

The stream that appeared as separate spills its boundaries and flows into the rivers of light, no longer needing to know itself as self, as other, as apart. Separation dissolves in the light of oneness. The totality of our light force ignites a massive conflagration and that which we have believed ourselves to be disappears, consumed in the fire of transformative love that is all that exists.

Meditation: Steeping in Satori

In this moment let go of every other moment that has ever been. Be here, right now.

Focus all your energy into NOW......and watch as each moment unfolds before you, without you having to do anything at all...

You are. Life is. That's it.

Let everything else fall away.

Satori.

Bliss.

Unlimited access to all that is.

Feel it. Know it. Be it.

There is nothing to do and nowhere to go. You are life and life is you and it is all Divine and utterly perfect.

Feel the twin threads of magenta and gold infusing your being and soar, dive, float, be.

Awaken. You are home.

Satori.

Satori in Action

Though I could offer you the words of those who have experienced *Satori* there is no experience of another that would tell you or show you what satori is. It is simply to be experienced. It simply is. May you discover it for yourself.

Key of Keys

As we travel deeper inside the seven gateways opened for us by our Golden Keys we discover that there is one overlighting key, a Key of Keys, a central theme and it is this: the letting go of control.

If we look closely we discover that the places in our life and on our journey where we struggle are the places where we fear to let go of control. Revisit our journey for a moment. Pause and reflect on each stopping point along the way, each place where the wheels got stuck in the mud; each time the journey seemed untenable because of the rain, the thunder, the storms; each path that seemed to peter out just as we placed our foot upon it. Take a closer look. What were we really afraid of? What were we trying to control?

Fear. Control. Two sides of the same tarnished coin. It's an old game this one. Do we really want to play it any more?

Every step of this journey is a choice. Faith asks us from the very beginning to trust and to assert our right as creative beings. Faith tells us: 'You' are not in control! Trust in the higher intelligence that is the source of all knowledge and the fountain of all life. From the beginning of our journey we are asked to relinquish control and to flow on a tide of trust in the infinite wonder of our life-force. Turquoise takes our cares and cleans them, soothes them, offering us a fresh perspective on all that has gone before.

Cleansed and refreshed, we begin to float out into the cool pale blue-lilac sea of impeccability. We steep in the stillness of our vastness and we are given the opportunity to offer up struggle, to release agitation, to forgo difficulty. When we let go of memory, inspiration is given a free rein. When we let go of control, angels gather to deliver exactly that which we would desire. The touch is light. The air is soft. Magic abounds.

Into this space of enchanted stillness the coral light of dawn emerges bringing with it the warmth, generosity and joy of the sun. As generosity's rays touch us, we begin to realise there is nothing to fear, that all is well and will always be well. We blossom, we unfurl and our hearts catch the light of the sun and ignite a gentle glowing flame of delight. What was it that we had hoped to control after all? The sun? The moon? The wind?

We are master manifestors, we know how to issue forth the arrow of a thought and watch it dart back to us as outcome. We may harness the creative power of our beingness to procure a situation, an event, an object of our desire. In so doing, we gather gently and swiftly the resources that are available to us and we lightly attune them with our thought-beams. We resonate and they connect and we entrain them to us, as easily as reaching out and picking up a leaf that has fallen at our feet. There is no effort here. No trying. We are and it is. Control's game is almost done.

I AM. In golden ringing tones we proclaim our 'amness' and watch as the dawn of our true power draws to the surface that which is not. We stand on the brink of our greatness and yet we decide, one last time, to continue to play by at least some of control's rules. We find old family patterns reaching out to draw us back into their folds. We watch as others resent or defy the power we know ourselves to be. We stand by as our addictive tendencies rear up before us one last time. Am I? Or am I not? Do I need control any longer? Gold's incisive brilliance slices through the centre of our game. We can either play, or leave. We look over our shoulder one last time and then, in I AM's golden embrace, we quit the race that has no winner.

We fall into grace's loving arms. Here there can be no control, here all is surrender. We gurgle and sigh like contented infants in the warmth of pink mother love. What, we ponder, was that thing we used to do? Surely we didn't try to manage, to direct, to manipulate? What on earth would have been the point! We slumber, sated and replenished on love's bounty and wonder at the perfection of all of life.

The ringing tone of the Ascension Light calls us to awaken. It is pure crystalline light and it is our light and it is our sound. And awaken we do. To the knowing of who we are. Divine light. Divine echoes. Uncontrolled and uncontrollable. Perfect. Joy-filled. Exquisite diamonds.

We ring and we sing and we emanate our living light across galaxies. We are home and untrammelled and every last piece of that which we would attempt to control falls away, crumbling into the magenta light of the Divine. This is satori.

Control curls up its toes and dissolves in the mighty fire of life.

What Now?

We shall not cease from exploration
And the end of all our exploring
Will be to arrive where we started
And know the place for the first time

~ T S Eliot

We have danced the golden dance and travelled through doorways and opened previously locked facets of our being. We have explored and delved and questioned and we have journeyed far. But this is not a fairytale (although on one level it is exactly that) and this is not a fairytale ending. When once we experience satori, we might wonder 'what now'? How do we live all that the Golden Keys would show us?

As embodiments of Divine source light experiencing itself we quest and thirst for new experiences, for new games, for ever-higher learning. We seek to evolve, we seek to know, we seek to experience. How will we know that what we are experiencing is real unless we experience it in everyday life? Only in the doing, only in the being can we know it.

How do we live our faith? We live our faith by choosing it, consciously, all the time. We live it by asking ourselves in each moment, in each situation, how it would look if we were in faith. We live it by living it. There is no other way.

How do we live impeccability? By constantly reminding ourselves of the perfection we are and life is. By being compassionate with ourselves, knowing that first, before all else, comes our alignment with ourselves, our greater truth, our higher light. We live impeccably by reaching into the waiting light of silence and pausing long enough to hear the voice of our inspired beingness.

How do we live generosity? We live generosity by returning to faith and remembering that there is always enough, that we are enough. We live generosity by giving and receiving impeccably and consciously. We live generosity by joining the dance of life and sounding the note that only we can make. We live generosity by opening to the interconnections of the web of life and recognising that what affects one affects all.

How do we live I AM? By choosing to be who we are, all of the time. By opening to a far greater, much vaster view of ourselves than we have ever dared to conceive. We live our I AM by balancing the awesome might of our power with the golden flame of love.

How do we live in grace? We surrender every thing in our lives and every second of our day and every cell of our being to the Divine that is all of life.

How do we live our Ascension Light in a body, on Earth? We claim the I AM and the power and wisdom of gold and we amplify it in the clear white light of our vastness. We draw the infinite wonder of divinity through our veins with our every breath. We consciously choose to know light, to be light, to live light, to connect with the light within and all around us. We look at everyone and everything and we choose to see them as light, we choose to see them in all their magnificently crafted perfection.

How do we live satori? We live satori as a small child, each moment unfolding in the awe and mystery and wonder of life. We live satori by constantly showing up in the ever-present now. We live satori by being all that we are.

The Ascension journey is a journey of consciousness, of awareness, of opening; it is a journey of expansion, evolution and unfolding. When we open the channels of our awareness we find reminders of our innate divinity at every turn. We use whatever tools and resources and words inspire us in the moment.

We are gifted once again with choices. We can choose satori every moment: Before enlightenment, chop wood, carry water. After enlightenment, chop wood, carry water. The journey now becomes about how we chop the wood, about the attitude with which we do it. We can recognise that satori is in the chopping, is the chopping. Chopping wood just is. Life is. We are. I am.

The magenta energy of *Satori* is of love for the moment, love in the little things, love in the detail, as well as in the allness. We are offered access to satori whatever the everyday nuances of life, the shocks, difficulties or challenges. Can we live faith, live impeccability, live generosity under all circumstances? Can we stand in our power, in our grace, in our light and know ourselves as all that is?

When we choose faith moment by moment we can choose satori moment by moment. With faith in every moment, we can have bliss in every moment. Faith keeps us in satori and satori offers us impeccable faith. The ending of our journey is but the beginning. The moment we are not in memory, the moment we are at 'zero', we are free to choose. And that is our journey. We just keep choosing.

What now? What do we want to do? Where do we want to go? Who do we want to be? How do we want to view life? All of it comes back to choices. The Golden Keys to Ascension reconnect us with our own Divine innate knowing, open us to the ringing of our soul's joyous truth. Our ever-willing heart and our ever-knowing soul offer us the possibility of transmuting what has kept us from choosing faith, choosing satori, choosing what is. In the purity and precision of the existing moment we are free to choose again, to choose according to our highest light, our deepest truth, our boundless ascending spirit.

The Language of Light

Language of Light

From The Mayan Oracle by Ariel Spilsbury and Michael Bryner (www.holographicgoddess.com)

Qualities: gateway, direct access, transmissions, feelings, preparation for ascension, transcendent consciousness

This lens heralds your approach to an interdimensional gateway. Be watchful – the language of light, the energy of your God Self, is assisting you in the crafting of your light body. This loving creation occurs through subtle transmissions of energy that can be sensed as pulses of light, color, sound or heightened vibration.

Trust and develop this sacred language. It is encoded in your feelings. You will know when you have a sudden sense of union, transcendence, or expanded perception. Learn to use your feelings as your spiritual steering mechanism. Let your heart be your compass. Allow this ancient mode of communication to spark memories of your purpose and destiny.

Symbols act as a means for decoding this abstract language. You do not have to 'understand' symbols; their meaning affects you on a supraconscious level that permeates all aspects of your being. Rather than relying on meanings fixed in memory, be receptive to your innate responses to symbols and metaphors. Let them ignite your own mythic coding, acting as a 'rapid transit' between realities. Colors are also part of this language. Notice and work with the colors that strongly attract you.

Remember, you are the knower. Fly into the pure state of consciousness where there are no words. Open to receive your native tongue, the galactic language of light. Feel the pulse of reunion, lovingly tendered as a gift of grace.

The Language of Light Transmitted

It is not yet 4am and already growing gently towards day. I've been receiving a stream of information and insight for about an hour when I'm drawn back to the Mayan Oracle card set and in my half-awake state, I knock them over. One card falls face up. It is the card called Language of Light. Again and again since that first time in South Africa, this card has shown up and I begin to ponder: who knocked them over? Was it an angel or a guide, helping me to remember the purpose of this book as I write it? Was it my own Higher Self, that part of me still utterly connected to my own Divine essence, to Source itself? Was it merely chance or fate? Is there some giant hand guiding my path from above or am I, as creator, exactly that? Am I my own giant hand?

As my link to Source gets clearer and stronger, I am more able to access the signs and signals sent out by my Source-self, the signals that guide the 'me' that is experiencing human life. I am more attuned to the subtleties of my soul's own language and more adept at translating them into my daily life. From the beginning I have felt that the purpose of this book is to transmit information, energy and knowledge through the Language of Light, this language we seem to know deep inside our cells but which we have forgotten on a conscious level. It is a language without words yet carried upon them. It is a language of energy, of concentrated light. It is a language that is universal. Borders and cultures make no difference. We all speak it, we all know it, we all resonate with its symbols and its kinetic messages.

The Language of Light is a transmission of transcendent consciousness, available to all who wish to access its golden call. Fall not into the weakened transience of your half-light but open to the greatness of your gifted full-hearted glory. Awaken now and be still. Let the whispers of the dawn carry their messages to your waiting soul. Arise and be the fulfilment of that of which you have dreamed. You are traversing now a new highway, a higher way, a lighter way. Travel on these new-found light-paths of joy and let their luminescent webs form patterns of delight within and before you. Lift your eyes to the curving arch of the waiting gateway and hesitate no longer. Go generously into the light of your soul and speak there only of love. There is no other time. All things are come. Divinity is yours. Life is the gift you are offered.

Will you receive it?

Appendices

1

Golden Words

The writing of this book is truly one of the most fascinating experiences of my life to date and it all begins during that week in South Africa with Melissie. We have spent four or five days on her terrace, gazing at the new golden bottles and allowing thoughts and insights to form. I've taken notes on a laptop and I'm beginning to wonder where they will lead.

Six days into my week-long odyssey with gold, I bath in white and gold *Ascension Light* and afterwards, words begin to organise themselves as I pull together the threads of the notes I have made. A voice begins to make itself heard, words appear on the screen in front of me and though I am very much involved in the process I feel at all times as though I am being guided, nudged and offered exactly the words I need. I've been asked several times if the material in this book is channelled information and if so, who I am connecting with as I write. I reply that what I write is spoken with my voice, through me and of me, and yet at the same time it comes from somewhere else altogether greater, vaster; that part of 'me' that is no longer an individual being but part of the great cosmic allness. I feel a team of what I can only describe as 'Light Writers' around me; beings who support and guide me as I write, and the essence of the book itself has a potent and defining presence.

At times, such as during the writing of the Harmonics for each Key, the voice I hear, feel, attune with becomes stronger, more insistent, takes on a different tone or frequency. I am somewhat astonished at the effect the words of these Harmonics have on those who hear or read them. Energy shifts, thrumming and shaking in the body, pulsing waves of energy, 'downloads', even darts of pain or discomfort are all common. Often, if I ask for feedback, I am told there are no words to describe what is being experienced. They seem to take the listener or reader into a unique and very different energetic space and I realise that something quite potent is being revealed through them though what that is I may not yet fully understand.

On my return to England I embark on three intensive months of teaching workshops. Alongside them, whenever time permits or when I feel the book calling me, I begin to develop the themes of the seven Keys and to write the introductory chapters. It is not until my first *Golden Keys to Ascension* courses begin in early June 2009 that work on the book begins in earnest. I know I will write one Key per week so that I can present each chapter to the two groups I am facilitating in time for them to connect with that particular Key for the week.

At the groups' weekly two-hour meetings we explore each Key and share feedback on the previous one. These classes often inspire me and over the next day or two I find myself jotting notes and insights, sometimes in the early hours of the morning. At some stage over the following days I become aware of what I can only describe as downloads: an initially subtle energy entering my crown, my heart or my body as a whole. Surges of varying intensity begin fizzing and buzzing around my being. As the energies ramp up I begin to feel incredibly tired and long to lie down. For anything from twenty minutes up to an hour or two the download continues then slowly ebbs. Afterwards, I always feel refreshed and revitalised and I soon begin to realise these energetic infusions are preparing me for the writing that is to come.

During each week as I connect with the bottle and the Key I find little inclination to do anything else. For the period of seven or eight weeks during which I am most intensively writing, nothing else really seems of much significance. I let go of teaching other workshops, stop seeing clients and immerse myself in the sheer wonder and joy of this process.

Six months after the initial visit to Melissie I find myself back in South Africa, called once again though I don't know exactly why. It feels completely aligned and in tune with the resonance of the book for me to finish the process begun six months before by returning to the source. I know that there are deeper layers of information still to be included in the book and they do indeed come to light as we spend another week together in the company of the Golden Keys. I am also called by the whales who come to the part of the Cape where Melissie lives for several months each year. Their magnetic pull is a defining reason for my journey back to South Africa and I am richly rewarded by their presence and the energetic shifts and transmissions I experience as they connect with me.

As Melissie and I explore the complementary colours to each of the Golden Gaia bottles I find myself asking her to make a bottle that is complementary to the gold and turquoise of *Faith*. Its beauty tumbles straight into my heart and I bath in this bottle of pale coral over pale blue-lilac after watching an African sunset laid out before me in exactly the colours of the bottle. Pouring the oil into the bath I notice small perfectly formed globes of clear liquid light which look like nothing so much as cells. This one does its work 'underground' as it were – I cannot put into words the shift that happens within me nor exactly how or why it is necessary. All I know is that it is the beginning of the next phase of information for me and for this book.

Two days later after a rich heart connection with the whales, I bath in the complementary colours to the *Generosity* bottle - pale turquoise over pale blue-lilac -and know that the next level of information is no longer 'out there' - it is on its way. I am infused with exquisite strands of light that I have been waiting for all my life. The book begins to speed its way to completion.

Home once again and an intensive period of editing begins, each draft taking me deeper into the magical weave of golden threads. I am eating, breathing, sleeping, living the Golden Keys and have truly never felt so blessed. I am humbled and honoured and excited by the richness of this journey and all I know for certain is that the best is yet to come.

I am learning more about myself and who I am through this process than anything I have done before. What I am discovering is that when we are shown ourselves, our true selves, in the mirror - whether that mirror be another person, a situation, or a potent bottle of coloured oil - what we are shown is so vast, so beyond logic, so expansive that it blows the rational mind. Quite simply, the golden rays of light I am exposed to during the writing of this book show me to myself so potently that I can no longer pull back, hide or shrink from the truth of who I am or what I am here to do.

I wish such blessings to all who read these words.

2

The Golden Keys to Ascension Eight-Week Programme

If you would like to experience the full delight of the Golden Keys, an eight-week course designed to facilitate and support your journey is offered by myself, Melissie Jolly and Moira Bush. Currently Moira and I are UK-based and Melissie is in South Africa.

Over the eight weeks of your programme, you will attend one two-hour class per week, bath in the sumptuous golden oils at your convenience, use the accompanying Angel essences to support your process and work with this book and guided daily reflections and practices. Reflective exercises engage your mind and indeed all aspects of the greater whole that makes you who you are. There is a fairly general consensus among those who have attended this programme so far: it is life-changing!

You can visit our websites for further details:

Korani (www.korani.net)
Melissie Jolly (www.colourmirrors.com)
Moira Bush (www.moirabush.com)

For those who are unable to attend a course in person a downloadable e-course and audio version of the programme is currently being developed.

For details visit www.korani.net and www.goldenkeys.ning.com

Ascension Packs

There are two Ascension Packs available. In Pack One you will find the seven Golden Gaia oils, the Gold Angel essence and this book.

Pack Two consists of the book, the same seven oils and seven coloured Angel essences, one for each corresponding Key.

Together, these are potent and utterly holistic packages. The oils are a practical delight for your physical body, taking the messages of the Keys right to the cells. The essences open, expand and enhance your energy bodies. The book offers transmissions to carry the energy and information of the Golden Keys to your being.

To order your Ascension Pack visit Korani Light Centre at www.korani.net

3

Korani's Colour Journey

I first met Colour Mirrors at the very beginning of 2005 when I interviewed Moira Bush for an article in a local holistic magazine. Moira was the first practitioner and teacher of Colour Mirrors in the United Kingdom and my meeting with her and the system quite frankly blew me away. I couldn't wait to know more. I had spent some time poring over the images of the bottles on the Colour Mirrors website in preparation for the interview and had recognised, with something approaching awe, the power of the system. I had also recognised a calling, an irrepressible excitement and a knowing deep within myself that this was my next step.

I had trained in NLP, Reiki, Reconnective Healing and Natural Nutrition and had set up a healing practice in 2003. I was being guided, quite definitely and assuredly, along my spiritual path. When I met Colour Mirrors, it was as if some knowledge, some instinct deep inside me was re-awoken. I knew this system and its many facets on a very potent level, though I had never come across it before, at least in this lifetime.

During 2005 I immersed myself in Colour Mirrors, incorporating the glorious colours into my healing work, offering readings using the system, and training as a Colour Mirrors teacher. I also met Melissie Jolly for the first time that year. Melissie and her teaching, wisdom and knowledge have touched me on a level that exceeds anything else I have yet experienced. My love for the system which was birthed through her, and indeed for this marvellous person herself, grows day by day. I am honoured to have been inducted as a trainer of Colour Mirrors teachers in 2007 and to walk alongside Melissie in the ongoing evolution of this incredible system. We watch in awe as it takes us where it will.

4

References

Louise Langley: The Ahquilieah Chronicles, The Flight of the Eagle. Permission granted by the author www.louiselangley.com

Philippa Merivale, Colour Works © 2005, Laramar Ltd. www.metatronic-life.com

Peggy Black, Multidimensional Channel, Transducer, Scribe and Witness. From Morning Messages, with permission www.morningmessages.com, 831-335-3145. peggyblack@aol.com

Ariel Spilsbury and Michael Bryner, The Mayan Oracle, Bear & Company Publishing, © 1992. Permission granted by Ariel Spilsbury: www.holographicgoddess.com

Melissie Jolly (from various transcribed conversations with the author and Colourworks newsletter 2007) www.colourmirrors.com

Philippa Merivale, Rescued by Angels © 2009, Reprinted by permission of O Books, www.o-books.net

Patrick Overton, The Leaning Tree (1975), Reprinted by permission of the author, www.patrickoverton.com

The Four Agreements © 1997, Miguel Angel Ruiz, M.D. Reprinted by permission of Amber-Allen Publishing, Inc. P. O. Box 6657, San Rafael, CA 94903. All rights reserved.

Joe Vitale and Ihaleakala Hew Len, Zero Limits, © Hypnotic Marketing and Dr Ihaleakala Hew Len (2007). Reprinted with permission of John Wiley & Sons, Inc.

The Art of Spiritual Peacemaking © James F. Twyman, 2003/2006. Passage from page 50 reprinted with permission of the Publisher. Published by Findhorn Press, Scotland.

The Magic of Believing, Claude M. Bristol (1948), Pocket Books.

One Taste © 2000 by Ken Wilber. Reprinted by arrangement with Shambhala Publications Inc., Boston, MA. www.shambhala.com

The Path of the Mystic, Osho (1988) Rebel Publishing.

Brian Johnson, from Philosophers Notes, with permission
www.PhilosophersNotes.com

T S Eliot (1942), Excerpt from poem: Little Gidding

5

Sources of Inspiration

There are many, many sources of inspiration, wisdom and insight available to us. The following websites and books have all been particularly bright beacons for me personally and have played a part in my evolutionary journey.

For useful and detailed information about the Ascension process I highly recommend Karen Bishop's books and her website:
www.emergingearthangels.com

Celia Fenn offers wonderful support and guidance for the Ascension process on her website www.starchildglobal.com

Peggy Black's Morning Messages are a great source of connection and wisdom: www.morningmessages.com

You may also like to visit www.lightworker.com for empowering information and guidance.

The following books are all powerful instruments for guidance and wonderful reminders of who we really are:

The Mayan Oracle by Ariel Spilsbury and Michael Bryner
(www.holographicgoddess.com)

Zero Limits by Joe Vitale (www.zerolimits.info)

The Four Agreements by Don Miguel Ruiz (www.miguelruiz.com)

Stepping Into The New Reality by Karen Bishop
(www.emergingearthangels.com)

Stillness Speaks by Eckhart Tolle (www.eckharttolle.com)

A New Earth by Eckhart Tolle (www.eckharttolle.com)

Loving What Is by Byron Katie (www.thework.com)

The Gentle Art of Blessing by Pierre Pradervand
(www.vivreautrement.org)

The Art of Spiritual Peacemaking by James Twyman
(www.emissaryoflight.com)

The Eight Human Talents by Gurmukh Kaur Kalsa
(www.goldenbridgeyoga.com)

The Pleiadian Workbook by Amorah Quan Yin
(www.amorahquanyin.com)

Awakening into Oneness by Arjuna Ardagh (www.livingessence.com)

An Ascension Handbook by Tony Stubbs (www.livingwithsoul.com)

Radical Forgiveness by Colin C. Tipping (www.radicalforgiveness.com)

The Essenes: Children of the Light; and Power of the Magdelene, both by
Joanna Prentis and Stuart Wilson
(www.foundationforcrystalchildren.com)

The Hathor Material by Tom Kenyon (www.tomkenyon.com)

The Reconnection by Eric Pearl (www.thereconnection.com)

The Work We Were Born To Do by Nick Williams
(www.inspired-entrepreneur.com)

Messages from Water by Masaru Emoto (www.hado.net)

Acknowledgements

Without Melissie Jolly, none of this would have happened. My gratitude and appreciation to you, Melissie, are eternal. It's that simple.

A huge thank you to the first groups to experience the *Golden Keys to Ascension* programme. You are a gift beyond words and your courage and commitment are awesome to behold. Thanks to all those who willingly gave feedback so that others may share your insights and experiences.

Grateful heart-felt thanks to my incredible friend Claire Farran for all your love, support and the sheer joy you bring into my life. Huge thanks to Amanda Ard and Sharon King for your marvellous insights, support and companionship on this journey. Many thanks to Sarah Cowell, Paddy Yorkstone and Clara Apollo for your encouragement, assistance and much-valued friendship. Grateful thanks to Sue Gleny for sterling proof-reading. Thanks to Pippa Merivale for being a guide and an awesome teacher. Thanks to Adele Robertson for years of thought-provoking and wonderful conversations which have contributed to my journey in countless ways. Hugs and untold gratitude to my beloved husband Darryl for just being your gorgeous grounded self. I couldn't do this without you, nor would I want to. I'm also profoundly grateful to the cosmic support and guidance that has been ever-present during the creation of this book and most of all to the ever-loving grace of the Divine.

About the Author

Korani is a workshop leader, facilitator and guide on the Ascension pathway. She offers seminars and workshops on, among other things, Ascension, colour, light, energy and human potential. Born in New Zealand, Korani now lives with her husband near Salisbury in the United Kingdom. Her passions include writing, travelling, walking, being in nature, heart-connections with joyful and light-minded beings, sunlight, starlight, light in general and increasingly, just being.